OUT OF EGYPT

Into Promise

David Ravella

OUT OF EGYPT

Into Promise

Advantage
BOOKS

DAVID RAVELLA

First Printing: July 2020
20 21 22 23 24 25   10 9 8 7 6 5 4 3 2 1
Printed in the United States of America

Table of Contents

David Ravella

Introduction

There are untold treasures to be discovered deep beneath the Bible's surface, an infinite mine of invaluable resources. Its worth cannot be estimated by earthly means or measures, nor its value determined through the appraisals of men. All of which, when happened to be found, can be traced back to one eternal source.

This supply is one that derives from above and only revealed when fixing our eyes on elements unseen. It is one of wisdom and understanding, a heavenly trove of knowledge and truth. More specifically, and most importantly, this indescribable treasury is Christ Himself.

Out of Egypt, Into Promise will set its gaze on one gem in particular, an underlying theme of redemption that perpetually seeks to surface: the Israelites' exodus out of Egypt is the model of salvation for all who accept Jesus as Lord.

Upon reading, you'll see how the ransom of Christ is the golden vein that runs through and through. The cornerstone of all supporting revelation; the focal point of all connecting imagery. From the Israelites' deliverance from Pharaoh to our exodus from sin and the devil, The Lamb slain from the foundation of the world is the promise in which our hope rests.

You may ask, *"how do the children of Israel relate to me?"* Or, *"what is the benefit of seeing Jesus within Exodus?"* Well, firstly, the Israelites relate to us much more than you may have thought. Secondly, seeing Jesus within the book of Exodus is why it was written in the first place. And not Exodus only, but *every* chapter of *every* book in the Bible.

From Genesis to Revelation, Jesus is the main attraction! However, if we are not intentional in seeking Jesus within each book, He'll remain behind the scenes. To those who seek, find; and to those who knock will be welcomed in. This book will not relent in its primary objective, nor deviate from the task at hand: unveiling the glory of Christ. In turn, we are changed into His same image (2nd Corinthians 3:18).

This book will help you take your eyes off your failures and to focus on His perfection. To find ourselves, we must find Him. Therefore, seeking Jesus in His word is to discover yourself in the first place. For as He is, so are we. Understanding our newfound identity will be the key to our inheritance.

Within Exodus specifically, we find the Lord's intervention into the bleakest of circumstances, one of hopelessness and fear. The children of Israel were Pharaoh's slaves with no way out! In response, the Lord raised up Moses as a deliverer who foreshadowed the One to come. Likewise, we had no way out of our deep-seated despondency. We were altogether hopeless! Understanding what Jesus truly delivered us from will propel us forward in abundant joy and lasting peace.

Had the Israelites seen Jesus within their departure from Egypt, their story would have ended differently. They would have triumphed in the wilderness rather than wander and would have inherited Canaan rather than perish. For this cause, their rebellious account was recorded so that we would *not* do what they did.

Nevertheless, there is a spotless model to be discovered. One that appears when exposed to the light. One that can be seen beyond the insolence and that can be heard above the complaints. Uncovering Christ's example hidden within the Old Testament will shed light on the path, purpose and destination of our journey.

From the flood of Noah to the curse of Canaan; From the sand and the stars to Isaac's birth; From the door post covered in blood, to the baptism through the Red Sea: It is God's many fingerprints left behind to be identified. From the manna, the grapes, the milk and the honey, to the giants trespassing in our inherited mountains; From the golden instruments to the priestly ceremonies; From the Tent of the Testimony to the Ark itself: Christ is the bright and exceeding glory to be unveiled.

Jesus is the gold at the surface, and the treasure beneath. He is the journey, the destination, and all that's in-between. After reading *Out of Egypt, Into Promise*, you'll undoubtedly see that a revelation of Christ is all you truly need.

Chapter One

Attention

"...Come ye, and let us go up to the mountain of the LORD, to the house of the God of Jacob..." (Isaiah 2:3)

It is difficult to see the forest from the trees, but apparent from atop the mountain. To understand our current position, we must ultimately gain a heavenly perspective. We have inherited the higher ground. Understanding our gifted position in Christ will be the key to our success.

In this first and foundational chapter (*Attention*), we begin our journey at the summit. From this vantage point, we can see the promised land ahead. From this height, even the deepest valley becomes plain to see in the overall view.

In order to grasp being seated in the heavens with Christ, and our feet gracing the earth simultaneously, we must allow His word to transform our minds. It is by embracing the Lord's original intent found in scripture that we may truly succeed in our relationship with Him. It is the sum of this writing in full.

This chapter will focus on the motive behind our study of the Bible. If we don't know *why* we are reading, we may aimlessly wander the wilderness. To arrive in the promised land, we must fully embrace the finished work of Christ.

Upon reading, you'll find three solid pillars that support all the following chapters. The purpose of God's word, our identity in Christ, and His goodness. Each pillar relies on the other to stand.

The *purpose* of the word is to change the way we think. Understanding the word's intention, and the correction it brings forth will set our crooked paths straight towards the promised land.

Our *identity* is found in seeking Christ's example. Like children pick up the habits of their parents, so will we grow into the shoes of our Father.

God's *goodness* is revealed in the very nature of Jesus. From this, we can rightly divide the thievery of the devil, and the abundant life granted by God.

Like Genesis precedes Exodus in the Bible, so will this chapter prepare us for what's to come. We need to understand the tools we have at hand, so we don't misuse or abuse them. *Attention* will equip you for the journey ahead. Knowing where you start is just as important as knowing where you are going.

Admonition

> *"Now all these things happened unto them for ensamples [examples]: and they are written for our **admonition**, upon whom the ends of the world are come." (1ˢᵗ Corinthians 10:11) (emphasis and brackets mine)*

The scripture above is an admonition of Paul on behalf of the children of Israel. In almost every book of the Bible, the children of Israel are mentioned or used as an example.

As any good parent would administer correction and instruction towards their children, so much more would our Father in heaven towards us. The Lord has given us His word and His Spirit to do so. Our natural parents may not have always done it right, but our Father has always had the best in mind for us.

> *"For they verily for a few days chastened [instructed] us after their own pleasure; but he for our profit, that we might be partakers of his holiness." (Hebrews 12:10 (brackets mine))*

Isn't it interesting how God calls the Israelites the *children* of Israel? This relates to us greatly. For all who accept Christ as Lord become the children of God.

How does a parent get the attention of their child?

"Samuel, Samuel…"

"Martha, Martha…"

"Simon, Simon…"

The Lord uses His word to get our attention, and more often than not, He repeats Himself.

It is extremely significant when scripture is repeated and should be highly regarded. Consider the Lord speaking to Joshua: He commanded him to be strong and courageous four times in the first chapter of the book! (Joshua 1:6-7, 9, 18).

In the epistle to the Galatians, Paul boldly proclaimed that if the apostles or even an angel from heaven were to preach another gospel, they should be cursed. He then repeated himself in the following verse.

In the book of Romans, between the sixth and seventh chapters, Paul used the phrase "God forbid" four times to drive home the importance of not living for the flesh, after being saved by grace.

Jesus said in Mark 4:3:

"Hearken; Behold, there went out a sower to sow."

He was emphasizing what was about to be addressed by saying hearken *and* behold in the same breath. *"Pay attention to this and understand, look!"*

When it comes to our admonition, the Lord repeats Himself for our benefit, so we do not make the same mistakes as our predecessors. At the same time, He calls attention to our Solution. Some scriptures shine a light on the way, while others spare us from destruction. All perfectly forged into one, sharp, double-edged sword.

The book of Proverbs comes to mind when considering admonition. It is the prime example of what a believer should follow and what they should avoid. It is the contrast between light and darkness, of wisdom and foolishness.

I can see the consequences of a man committing adultery, stealing, lying, deceiving, and manipulating people for his benefit, to heed as a warning. On the other hand, I can see the benefit of a man following God whole-heartedly, seeking to give rather than steal, and loving people with a pure and fervent heart, to be the example I follow.

The Lord doesn't want us touching the stove to find out it's hot. He would rather that we learn from those who've already burnt their own hands. Nevertheless, there is One worth focusing on entirely; One Who has walked completely unscathed.

"For whatsoever things were written aforetime were written for our learning, that we through patience and comfort of the scriptures might have hope." (Romans 15:4)

All these scriptures were written for our learning. They are all for our advantage. Who are we learning about? Jesus, of course. He is the Teacher *and* Subject of the book. Indeed, the modus of learning is repetition, and He is the resounding theme of the whole Bible.

Volume Of The Book

Psalm 40:7 says: *"Then said I, Lo, I come: In the volume of the book it is written of me."*

Therefore as we study the Bible, we're to seek the revelation of Christ within. It is the main reason we are reading the word to begin with. Whether in Genesis, or Numbers, whether in Job, or Hosea: discovering Jesus is our primary objective.

For example: If you had an encyclopedia collection numbered 1-66 and were to take away any one of those books, the collection would be incomplete. In fact, if you were to look at the bookshelf in where they were held, the missing volume would stand out the most! So, if anyone were to say the Old Covenant should be disregarded because it's been fulfilled, or how it's the law, and we're under grace, they would be in error. They would have missed the whole point… Jesus is the main subject!

The Old Covenant is the New Covenant *concealed*, and the New Covenant is the Old Covenant *revealed*, with Jesus in the center of it all.

> *"Ask, and it shall be given you; seek, and ye shall find; knock, and it shall be opened unto you: For every one that asketh receiveth; and he that seeketh findeth; and to him that knocketh it shall be opened."* *(Matthew 7:7, 8)*

Jesus is behind every door of passage in scripture. All we need is the desire to find Him because He always wants to be found.

Have you ever purchased a vehicle, and throughout the buying process, happen to see that exact model on the road everywhere you looked? How could this be? Truth be told, that particular car had always been on the road, you just hadn't set your attention on it alone.

I once found it similar in my approach to reading scripture. I may have been in the word at times to read casually or may have read stories of Bible characters, and found them interesting enough, but I wasn't seeking Jesus *alone* in scripture. Sure, I would occasionally see a foreshadow of Him in the Old Testament, and of course, I would see Him in the Gospels, but I only seemed to find Him when it was evident. But when He became the model I sought for in each book, He became all that I would see!

> *"And beginning at Moses and all the prophets, he expounded unto them in all the scriptures the things concerning himself."* *(Luke 24:27)*

This book's *purpose* is to bring about that reality… it's all about Him. He is revealed throughout the whole Bible… if we simply care to look.

Seeing Him for Who He truly is, will change us into who we truly are.

Lo, And Behold

"Or despisest thou the riches of his goodness and forbearance and longsuffering; not knowing that the goodness of God leadeth thee to repentance?" (Romans 2:4)

Knowing Jesus makes all the difference. He is not a list of do's and don'ts, or laws and regulations. He is the One and only living God who desires a relationship with His people. Once we were the children of darkness, but now the children of Light.

"In all thy ways acknowledge him, and he shall direct thy paths." (Proverbs 3:6)

The word acknowledge here is *yada*, which means: *to know*. It implies a relationship through intimacy, affection, and trust. It is the same word concerning sexual relations between a man and his wife:

"And Adam knew [yada] Eve his wife…" (Genesis 4:1 (brackets mine))

In the context of being intimate with Christ in His word: Knowing Jesus will produce an offspring of true and lasting change.

A misconception, and fruitless endeavor, is trying to have a change of action (based on self-will and effort) before a change of mind. This would be a dead work. The change of mind, or *metanoia* in Greek, is the fruit of the root: which is knowing Christ. We must first have a change of mind before any change in our actions.

"Bring forth therefore fruits meet for repentance. And now also the axe is laid unto the root of the trees: therefore every tree which bringeth not forth good fruit is hewn down, and cast into the fire." (Matthew 3:8, 10)

You can't bear fruit unless you are rooted in good ground. That ground is Christ.

Do you clean yourself up *before* you jump in the shower? As foolish as this question may sound, it makes all the difference. Obviously, the answer is no. The shower was created for cleansing. You come to the shower as you are, and the water does the work. Any work involved during the shower is *after* the water is applied.

> *"I indeed baptize you with **water** unto **repentance**..." (Matthew 3:11) (emphasis mine)*

Consider what John the Baptist said about Jesus' increase in his life:

> *"He must increase, but I must decrease." (John 3:30)*

This is a major statement! Imagine if the passage had been written like this: *"I must decrease, but He must increase."*

This would imply that only our work and effort would give place for Jesus' increase. This would also suggest that we would have to become small so that He could become big. This is not so. This kind of mentality will only frustrate a believer. We will find ourselves striving through self-will and human effort.

True change is not coming to the altar in emotion and confessing sin. How many altar experiences have you had where you've said to the Lord:

"This is the last time! I promise I will change and never do this again!" Only to find yourself at the altar again the next week, confessing the same thing you promised the Lord you'd stop doing. Confessing sin alone is not the way we change our minds: abiding in His word, and having Him be our focus, will change our mind *first*, followed by our actions.

What John the Baptist implied was this: Jesus' increase will automatically bring our decrease. It's only by beholding Him that we'll truly change in the first place.

> *"But we all, with open face **beholding** as in a glass the glory of the Lord, are **changed** into the same image from glory to glory, even as by the Spirit of the Lord." (2nd Corinthians 3:18) (emphasis mine)*

The word changed here is *metamorphoō*, which means: *to be transformed, transfigured, changed in form*. Notice also the order in which it is written: behold comes first and changed comes after. The same Greek word is used here for transformed:

*"And be not conformed to this world: but be ye **transformed** by the renewing of your mind, that ye may prove what is that good, and acceptable, and perfect, will of God." (Romans 12:2) (emphasis mine)*

To touch back on the passage from second Corinthians, it also says:

"Even by the Spirit of the Lord."

It is *only* by His Spirit that we can change.

"Then he answered and spake unto me, saying, This is the word of the LORD unto Zerubbabel, saying, Not by might, nor by power, but by my spirit, saith the LORD of hosts." (Zechariah 4:6)

"Can the Ethiopian change his skin, or the leopard his spots? then may ye also do good, that are accustomed to do evil." (Jeremiah 13:23)

Transformation is tied to understanding righteousness, which is our new identity. Beholding Him, and agreeing with what He has *already* done within, will produce lasting change. We cannot change our spots by looking at the spots themselves. We need to accept that He's already made us spotless within (within our born-again, righteous spirit). When we look to the Son, He becomes the increase that brings our effortless decrease. When we focus on our shortcomings, that increases, and we frustrate the grace of God.

If the Israelites would have beheld the Lord in the wilderness, rather than look back to Egypt, they would have inherited Canaan.

How do we behold Jesus? In the light of His word.

"And was transfigured before them: and his face did shine as the sun, and his raiment was white as the light." (Matthew 17:2)

The Lord Himself causes the metamorphosis of our minds as we behold Him. It is Jesus' face shining like the sun upon us that produces change. The devil knows the danger of us staring at the Son, that's why he tries his best to keep our heads down. We must resist this discouragement and lift them up! We ought to stare at the Son and go blind to everything else!

"Set your affection on things above, not on things on the earth." (Colossians 3:2)

True change is more of a metamorphosis than a confession of sin at the altar. We should come out of the cocoon a butterfly, not crawl out half a caterpillar.

Free Indeed

*"If the **Son** therefore shall make you free, ye shall be free indeed." (John 8:36) (emphasis mine)*

Are you truly free if you were released from jail, but afraid to go back? If your mind is on the jail cell you came out of, it cannot be on the promised land. You don't have to reside in a jail cell to be imprisoned physically, you can remain there in your mind just the same.

Condemnation and a sin-conscience will have you identifying with the prisoner you once were, rather than the born-again believer and child of God you are now.

When you were a sinner without Christ, you hardly thought of holiness, if ever at all! And if you thought of getting your act together, outside of Christ, it was impossible. Your *nature* was sin, and you were wholly submerged in its muck and mire. Like a fish in its natural habitat, so were you in the murky water.

However, you are now an eagle! To be concerned about the habitat of a fish is to disregard the open air of the eagle. An eagle is free indeed!

If an eagle were to fall in the water, it wouldn't make it a fish. It would just be a wet eagle. It wouldn't affect its nature. But to stay in the water, and to think like a fish, would most definitely affect its ability to fly.

*"**And such were some of you**: but ye are washed, but ye are sanctified, but ye are justified in the name of the Lord Jesus, and by the Spirit of our God." (1st Corinthians 6:11) (emphasis mine)*

The eagle's answer to its wet feathers would be to fly towards the Sun.

We are no longer stagnating in the polluted waters of sin, but in the open air of righteousness. We must identify with who we are now, and forsake all that was left behind (Philippians 3:13). For this cause, our conscience must be clear. It must be full of Christ, and void of condemnation.

Lay Aside The Weight

Mary says in the gospel of Luke: *"...My soul doth magnify the Lord."* Luke 1:46

Also, David, prophesying in the Psalms:

"My soul shall make her boast in the LORD: the humble shall hear thereof, and be glad. O magnify the LORD with me, and let us exalt his name together." (Psalm 34:2, 3)

This is imperative to understand: Our soul is like a magnifying glass, and we will either magnify, 1: The Lord, or, 2: *Whatever* else. Whatever we focus on becomes bigger. If we try to focus on our decrease, guess what? Whatever we're struggling with becomes greater. If we focus on Jesus, our soul will magnify Him!

I would like to bring to light a perspective of Hebrews, chapter 12, which may revolutionize your journey with Jesus.

"Wherefore seeing we also are compassed about with so great a cloud of witnesses, let us lay aside every weight, and the sin which doth so easily beset us, and let us run with patience the race that is set before us, Looking unto Jesus the author and finisher of our faith; who for the joy that was set before him endured the cross, despising the shame, and is set down at the right hand of the throne of God. For consider him that endured such contradiction of sinners against himself, lest ye be wearied and faint in your minds. Ye have not yet resisted unto blood, striving against sin." (Hebrews 12:1-4)

This passage is packed! One thing to note is how the beginning of this chapter starts with *wherefore*, which implied there were things written prior that validated what was said next. The theme of the book is about Jesus being our high priest, and how He perfected us once and for all, by offering Himself.

The writer then explains *how* to lay aside every weight and the sin that so easily trips us. He says *sin*: singular, not *sins*: plural. This is the key to unlocking the intended context of this passage. We all have sins that easily beset us.

For example, I may not struggle with being tempted by alcohol and becoming drunk, but my friend may experience frequent temptation. So, what besets my friend may not beset me. What hinders one person may not hinder another. However, the sin that hinders us all is *not* looking unto Jesus! This is what brings us all to a common ground. We may all fall into the sins that beset us by looking at the sin itself, but the sin that besets us all is not looking unto Jesus in the first place!

The writer says:

*"For **consider him** that endured such contradiction of sinners against himself, lest ye be wearied and faint in your minds." (Hebrews 12:3) (emphasis mine)*

Considering Him is our answer! He strove earnestly against sin, and His precious blood burst out from His forehead. His capillaries ruptured due to such strenuous prayer in Gethsemane (Hebrews 12:4). Where we gave over our peace and fell in our soul in the garden of Eden, Jesus took back in the garden of Gethsemane. He did this by subjecting His soul to His Father's will.

This garden (Gethsemane) is where Jesus would often resort back to (John 18:2). Where man used to walk in the garden with God, Jesus walked there often with His disciples. What a beautiful foreshadow of us being able to once again walk with God through Jesus!

Now, when we find ourselves tempted by the tempter, we consider Jesus' striving and resistance for us against sin. We were not built to handle the weight. So, we must lay it aside by looking unto Him alone.

"Casting all your care upon him; for he careth for you." 1ˢᵗ *Peter 5:7*

Furthermore, He was buried in a garden tomb. Where we died with Adam in the garden, Jesus was buried and rose again. He went back to where it all began, reclaiming all that was lost, and made it better. The Last Adam, and True Gardner, has made all things new!

Life In The Blood

Consider Jesus' resistance in the garden. When the blood from His forehead hit the ground, He reversed the curse of us: *"eating bread by the sweat of our face,"* and the ground being: *"cursed for our sake"* (Genesis 3:17, 19).

His righteous blood also set us free from the "thorns and thistles," when the crown of thorns given to Him was pressed into His skull.

"For the life of the flesh is in the blood: and I have given it to you upon the altar to make an atonement for your souls: for it is the blood that maketh an atonement for the soul." (Leviticus 17:11)

A revelation of the power of His blood will set you free in whatever area you find yourself striving. The blood of Jesus will also keep your heart pure towards God and without condemnation. The blood on the doorpost is what caused the death angel to pass over. The children of Israel weren't condemned because of the blood!

It's only by His blood that we: have a *new covenant* (Hebrews 9:16-18); have *new life* (John 6:53); are *sanctified* (Hebrews 10:10); are *perfected* (Hebrews 10:14); are *forgiven* (Ephesians 1:7); are *justified* (Romans 5:9); are *cleansed* from all sin (1st John 1:7); are *redeemed* (Ephesians 1:7); are *purged* and *purified* (Hebrews 1:3); are *righteous* (2nd Corinthians 5:20, Romans 10:10); can *draw near* to Him (Ephesians 2:13); have a *clean conscience* (Hebrews 9:14, 10:22); have *boldness* to enter in (Hebrews 10:19); have *confidence* (Ephesians 3:12); have *peace* (Colossians 1:20).

The blood of Jesus washed us white as snow and now enables us to stand in confidence before the God of Love. We have peace with God by the blood of His cross! Our past has been washed away, only to leave standing a brand-new creation. Our sins have been cast into the depths of the sea, where the Lord remembers them no longer (Micah 7:19, Isaiah 43:25, Hebrews 8:12). This is the gospel!

"As far as the east is from the west, so far hath he removed our transgressions from us." (Psalm 103:12)

Remember what happened after man fell in the garden of Eden? The Lord placed Cheribums with flaming swords to guard the tree of life. He positioned these angels at the east of the garden, where it all began! "as far as the east is from the west."

Jesus is the Tree of Life who was kept from man until the determined time of the Father. Now, we can eat of Him in our righteous state and live forever! Adam and Eve were kept from the tree of life after falling, but now we have the right to eat freely.

There's no longer a veil of separation, or angels yielding flaming swords; the blood of Jesus has made the way! This is vital to be convinced of in our walk with God so we may have a healthy relationship with Him. The shed blood of Jesus has given us confidence once more to walk with Him. So, don't condemn yourself, because He's not condemning you.

Continuing to identify with where we came from will hinder where God wants to take us. We will not blindly end up in the fullness of the land; we must permit Jesus to transform our minds. It is vital to stay focused on where we are going and imperative to understand where we started. This only occurs through an intimate relationship with His word.

Taste And See

Now that we have access to partake of the Tree of Life, we can taste and see that the Lord is good! Due to this newfound reality of Heaven within, we can now view God with a good perspective. In fact, the filter or lens in which we view Him *must* be good.

If I were to place invisible tape over my camera lens, and then draw on that tape with a blue marker, the picture would come out with a blue perspective. Some camera lenses may be colored grey, and others may be colored black. The point being, it is vital to have a picture of God with a clear perspective altogether.

In this example, our soul is that of a filter and a lens that has been colored on. Our soul has been tainted by the world's perspective and must be renewed by His word. We must allow what's transpired in our born-again spirit to flood into our soul.

This process is what we'll discuss throughout the course of this book. It is within this progression that we begin to see the reality of Heaven come forth in the earth. Our minds may be the only thing holding us back from possessing the fullness of our inheritance. Consider what's said in Psalm 19:7: *"The law of the Lord is perfect; converting the soul…"*

The word *convert* here means: *to turn back, recover, restore*. It is inferred towards recovering that which was lost. Restoring to (or better than) original. God's word will restore our soul to see Him the way we should have originally. Which is seeing Him through the lens of His goodness: Jesus Christ.

My theology is wholly founded on God being good. When I don't understand a scripture, or uncertain if I'm hearing the Lord correctly, I step back and become still. I remind myself that He's good, regardless of what I'm facing. This should be the basis of our belief system. Otherwise, when something seems to contradict His nature, we can allow our misinterpretation of that passage, or difficult circumstance, to pervert our view of the Lord.

"Knowing this first, that no prophecy of the scripture is of any private interpretation. For the prophecy came not in old time by the will of man: but holy men of God spake as they were moved by the Holy Ghost" (2nd Peter 1:20-21)

We have privately interpreted God's word through distorted lenses, and ultimately the wrong perspective of His nature to begin with. We have sought the Lord with worldly filters and have wondered if He is who He says He is. I assure you... He most certainly is.

"...for he that cometh to God must believe that he is, and that he is a rewarder of them that diligently seek him." Hebrews 11:6

Must believe He is what? Believe that He is good!

Some believer's view the Father in the way they were treated by their father. Some, who were mistreated or abused, have a hard time seeing Him as a God of love. Only the submersion in His word through the filter of His goodness will convert our minds to see Him clearly.

Jesus told Peter if he didn't allow Him to wash his feet, he wouldn't have part with Him. (I will cover this concept in greater detail in chapter four, *Bitter Waters*.) He related Peter's feet washing to our minds being washed by His word. For this cause, we must allow Jesus to wash our feet. We can't afford to develop perverted views of our Father based on the depravity of our unrenewed mind.

"And ye shall know the truth, and the truth shall make you free." (John 8:32)

We must lay down our perceived truths and only believe *the* truth. When we make room for the Holy Spirit to reveal the truth, it is then that our perceived truths change.

We have blamed God for tragedies that were orchestrated by the devil. And in other cases, we have accepted God as the One who introduces the tragedy, yet, "works all things together for good" (Romans 8:28). In other words, we accept sickness and lack as the Father's "good" way to teach us.

The scripture says:

"If ye then, being evil, know how to give good gifts unto your children, how much more shall your Father which is in heaven give good things to them that ask him?" (Matthew 7:11)

If we, being evil, want what's best for our children, how much more the giver of Life? What parent among you would place a *bad* sickness upon their precious child, to get a *good* result? In what world does this make sense? I assure you, not in this world, nor in the one to come. There is no sickness in the kingdom of God. Isn't that where we were translated in the first place: God's kingdom? What the Father placed upon Jesus on the cross, will never be taken back and placed upon us.

Jesus said it was finished. All sickness vanquished through Jesus' body will never be placed upon us by our good Father, ever. Let that sink deep within the depths of your soul. He will *never* place sickness upon your body.

In the natural, only a sadistic father would get pleasure out of the suffering of his children. That man would not be fit for raising them, and they should be taken into protective custody. Our Father has proven His goodness and His love for us in this: He gave His one and only Son (John 3:16).

Notice the other 3:16 passage found in the first book of John:

> *"Hereby perceive we the love of God, because he laid down his life for us: and we ought to lay down our lives for the brethren." (1st John 3:16)*

Our perception of God's goodness and love cannot be founded on how we feel, it was demonstrated on the cross. The cross of Jesus Christ has proven His love for us once and for all. You cannot be a God who *is* Love, and not *be* Good.

Do you Love me?

> *"Again, the kingdom of heaven is like unto treasure hid in a field; the which when a man hath found, he hideth, and for joy thereof goeth and selleth all that he hath, and buyeth that field." (Matthew 13:44)*

Concerning His goodness and His love, we must thoroughly understand value. It is the regard held by one who sees something to be of worth; it is the price someone is willing to pay.

Regarding the value God placed upon us, and the price that was paid, consider the sacrifice given. (Truly, a sacrifice must have worth. Otherwise, it is of no sacrifice at all.)

King David said:

"...Nay; but I will surely buy it of thee at a price: neither will I offer burnt offerings unto the LORD *my God of that which doth cost me nothing. So David bought the threshingfloor and the oxen for fifty shekels of silver." (2*nd *Samuel 24:24)*

He wouldn't offer sacrifice that wasn't at a cost!

Notice what Jesus said concerning the rich men and the widow:

"And he looked up, and saw the rich men casting their gifts into the treasury. And he saw also a certain poor widow casting in thither two mites. And he said, Of a truth I say unto you, that this poor widow hath cast in more than they all: For all these have of their abundance cast in unto the offerings of God: but she of her penury hath cast in all the living that she had." (Luke 21:1-4)

These rich men tithed of their abundance, which didn't cost them anything. They wouldn't have missed it at all, because they had plenty to spare; yet this poor widow gave the last of the little she had left. She gave more because it meant something to her. She didn't have anything left to give.

In Malachi, we're left with a rebuke from God concerning the hearts of the Jews in their vain and evil offerings. It would've been better had they not offered at all, then to have offered their diseased animals. Four hundred years later, the Lord would prove His heart by providing the unblemished Lamb of God.

"Ye offer polluted bread upon mine altar; and ye say, Wherein have we polluted thee? In that ye say, The table of the LORD *is contemptible. And if ye offer the blind for sacrifice, is it not evil? and if ye offer the lame and sick, is it not evil? offer it now unto thy governor; will he be pleased with thee, or accept thy person? saith the* LORD *of hosts...Ye said also, Behold, what a weariness is it! and ye have snuffed at it, saith the* LORD *of hosts; and ye brought that which was torn, and the lame, and the sick; thus ye brought an offering: should I accept this of your hand? saith the* LORD*." (Malachi 1:7-8, 13)*

The Jew's sacrifices were shameful and irreverent. Not only were they worthless, they were despised altogether; by the Jews, and by God Himself.

All this to say, consider the offering the Father gave: He didn't send a lame or a sick angel to die in His place... maybe one He wouldn't really miss. He didn't send His best angel... one that could still be replaced. He didn't ask a righteous man to die in His place. He didn't ask or send anyone else to do it. He didn't offer money; He didn't offer gold. He gave the most irreplaceable One of all: He gave Himself. There wasn't any more that He could give!

The epitome of Love, and the greatest sacrifice of all. For who? The apple of His eye. The joy set before Him. The ones He held in such high regard that He was willing to pay with His very own blood.

Jesus' sacrifice ultimately declares how valued, how loved, and how irreplaceable we are to Him. For this reason, we can no longer base our perspective of Him through any other lens. We must see Him for who He truly is. Our God is Good.

Chapter Two

Four Hundred Years

"As the winter provided regard for spring, so did the time of silence for Christ."

The depths and riches of His word are truly unsearchable. The Bible is the only book you can pick up from any chapter or verse within, and follow right along. You can stop and meditate upon one passage for hours, or you can choose to read line upon line, precept upon precept. You can start at Revelation and work your way back, or you can start "in the beginning." You can spend the next month comparing characters in the Bible in hopes of painting a complete picture of Jesus, or you can study His life directly in the gospels.

You can use an exhaustive concordance to find every passage where *faith* is mentioned and do a word study, or you can do a word study on the word "*word*." You can read one of the thirty-one chapters of Proverbs each day, and rejoice in the Lord through the Psalms.

The Bible speaks to the distinctive hearts of the young and the old, the male and the female alike. The Bible has all things for all people.

Are you a lover of history? You can read of the wars, and the rise and fall of kings and their kingdoms. You can read of the passion of the prophets, as they disregard their own lives through the bold rebuke of the wicked. Are you a lover of poetry? The books of wisdom (Job, Psalms, Proverbs, Ecclesiastes and Song of Solomon) are literary masterpieces.

You can dig as deep as you'd like, or you can be just as content on the surface. It is living, breathing, and inspired by God. Truly, the Bible is the Book of all books.

I recall playing hide and seek with my niece and nephews, and hearing them say:

"Here I am, come and find me! Come on Uncle David, I'm over here!"

They would get a little restless if I wasn't searching in the same room as them, and before long, they would reveal their location to me. They wanted to be found!

As we're in the water of God's word, He is playing Marco Polo with us. He's answering "Polo" to reveal His location because He wants to be found!

This chapter will focus on a few timeframes and comparisons that highlight the wisdom and glory of the word. We'll discuss what happened before the children of Israel exited Egypt, through the flood of Noah and the life of Abraham. We'll bring Jesus out in each example as the focus of our study.

It is written in hopes of igniting the wonder within so that you'd always read the Bible as a child. He has hidden Himself with the intent to be discovered. It's an ongoing game of hide and seek, where His hiding spots are never exhausted. There is *always* another spot where Jesus is waiting to be found.

Marco...?

Marco...?

Marco...? Polo!

Forty Days And Forty Nights

"These are the generations of Noah: Noah was a just man and perfect in his generations, and Noah walked with God." (Genesis 6:9)

The flood in Noah's age would altogether change the world. From the time of life to the earth's structure, everything would become new.

Within the ark Noah built were two of all the unclean animals above the sea, seven of every clean, eight human souls, and God Himself. This would be the start of the new world.

Astoundingly, before Noah and his family entered the ark, it hadn't yet rained from above. There was only a mist that went up from the earth beneath, that watered the face of the ground. Noah was building a boat on dry land, believing the Lord would bring the rain, though it had never rained before. This is faith, and faith pleases God.

"In the six hundredth year of Noah's life, in the second month, the seventeenth day of the month, the same day were all the fountains of the great deep broken up, and the windows of heaven were opened." (Genesis 7:11)

For forty days and forty nights, the fountains burst, and the heavens poured out. All flesh was destroyed, leaving only what was within the ark to survive. Consequently, the earth was dramatically altered after the flood.

As hot water and magma pierced through the ocean floor, the earth's continents rapidly separated. This would counter the theory of Pangea's effect (which claims the supercontinent slowly drifted apart for millions of years). Noah's flood was the cause of the earth's sudden drift, resulting in an ice age when settled.

Man went from living hundreds of years, to a maximum of one hundred and twenty. Even plant and animal life would undergo a shorter lifespan. The atmosphere in the time of Noah was much different than that of today. The earth was more of a hyperbaric chamber before the flood, which preserved and lengthened all life. It is immensely different than what it once was.

We are technically living in a "post-post-paradise." First, man was kicked out of paradise in Eden to roam the earth outside of it. Then, man stepped foot off the ark into the world as we now know it. The most beautiful destination this earth presently has to offer cannot be compared to the paradise man once lived in. We'll never know this side of heaven. Thank God for the new heaven and new earth to come!

Interesting to note, the waters held within the firmament above were there beforehand. Before man sinned and before Noah entered the ark, the waters were waiting to be poured upon the earth from heaven above. This speaks to me of the plan set in place through Christ before the worlds were formed:

*"And all that dwell upon the earth shall worship him, whose names are not written in the book of life of the **Lamb slain from the foundation of the world.**" (Revelation 13:8) (emphasis mine)*

Jesus was crucified before time began. The Father had salvation in mind before we ever decided to fall.

The waters above would baptize the earth:

"...and Noah only remained alive, and they that were with him in the ark" (Genesis 7:23)

Through baptism, only we are spared while everything else is destroyed.

"And Noah builded an altar unto the LORD; and took of every clean beast, and of every clean fowl, and offered burnt offerings on the altar. And the LORD smelled a sweet savour; and the LORD said in his heart, I will not again curse the ground any more for man's sake; for the imagination of man's heart is evil from his youth; neither will I again smite any more every living thing, as I have done." (Genesis 8:20, 21)

Noah stepped out of the ark into a brand-new world. Likewise, we have stepped into a brand-new life. Like Noah's sacrifice was accepted, so does the Lord accept Jesus' sacrifice. It is a sweet smell unto Him for Christ's sake!

Notice also how the Lord said He wouldn't curse the ground anymore. He says this *after* the flood. The wooden ark and the flood were symbolic of the cross of Jesus and the judgment He took for us. The flood was the funeral procession for our old man.

"Know ye not, that so many of us as were baptized into Jesus Christ were baptized into his death?" (Romans 6:3)

"Therefore if any man be in Christ, he is a new creature: old things are passed away; behold, all things are become new." (2nd Corinthians 5:17)

Noah, whose name means rest, was a great foreshadow of Jesus.

"And he called his name Noah, saying, This same shall comfort us concerning our work and toil of our hands, because of the ground which the LORD hath cursed." (Genesis 5:29)

Jesus would build an ark in the middle of our wickedness. He would spare us from judgment by having his ground (flesh) cursed in our stead. He would then take the flood of judgment upon Himself.

Cursed Be Canaan/Blessed Be Judah

"And the sons of Ham; Cush, and Mizraim, and Phut, and Canaan." (Genesis 10:6)

Post-flood: Noah and his family began to settle into their new world. We find that Noah's nakedness was exposed unto Ham, and his son Canaan was punished for it. Why wasn't Ham cursed for this? When Noah awoke from his drunkenness the next day, he cursed his grandson, Canaan!

"And Noah awoke from his wine, and knew what his younger son had done unto him. And he said, Cursed be Canaan; a servant of servants shall he be unto his brethren. And he said, Blessed be the LORD God of Shem; and Canaan shall be his servant." (Genesis 9:24-26)

Noah said: *"Cursed be Canaan."* Interestingly, the fourth-born son unto Ham paid the penalty for his father's sin. I believe this is truly significant when taking all things into consideration.

For one, the children of Israel spent four hundred years in Egypt or *four* generations.

Secondly, Canaan took the punishment in the place of someone else. The *land* of Canaan then became the children of Israel's promised land. Jesus, the *Man*, took the punishment for someone else: us. In turn, the promised land became habitable!

Furthermore, Jacob's fourth son was Judah. This would be the tribe that Jesus would come through. Judah was delivered through Leah, Jacob's wife.

"And when the LORD saw that Leah was hated, he opened her womb: but Rachel was barren." (Genesis 29:31)

Rachel was loved, but Leah was hated. The Lord greatly exalts the things that are despised. The Lord allowed Leah to have a hand in delivering Jesus! Isn't it like the Lord to root for the underdog? The Lord Himself is meek and lowly in heart.

"And base things of the world, and things which are despised, hath God chosen, yea, and things which are not, to bring to nought things that are." (1st Corinthians 1:28)

"...for the LORD seeth not as man seeth; for man looketh on the outward appearance, but the LORD looketh on the heart." (1st Samuel 16:7)

Jesus would be hated, despised, and rejected. For this cause: God, through Jesus Christ, would open the womb of salvation for all!

Judah's name means *praise*. Surely, we can praise God for such a wonderful salvation wrought through Jesus.

Canaan was cursed, Judah was blessed.

"Christ hath redeemed us from the curse of the law, being made a curse for us: for it is written, Cursed is every one that hangeth on a tree." (Galatians 3:13)

What I find amazing about the promised land is how it was never about a land to begin with. (We will discuss this in greater detail in the last chapter, *Into Promise*.) This promise is spoken forth consistently by God:

"In the same day the LORD made a covenant with Abram, saying, Unto thy seed have I given this land, from the river of Egypt unto the great river, the river Euphrates…And said unto me, Behold, I will make thee fruitful, and multiply thee, and I will make of thee a multitude of people; and will give this land to thy seed after thee for an everlasting possession." (Genesis 15:18, 48:4)

What's remarkable about these prophecies is how the seed is deemed the beneficiary of the promise. Through Abraham, the tribe of Judah, and King David, would come the promised Seed.

"And I will put enmity between thee and the woman, and between thy seed and her seed; it shall bruise thy head, and thou shalt bruise his heel." (Genesis 3:15)

There is no seed in a woman. The seed is in the man. Jesus was the Seed within Mary by the Holy Ghost.

If I may ask, what land can last forever? Abraham is told he would have this land *forever*:

"And I will give unto thee, and to thy seed after thee, the land wherein thou art a stranger, all the land of Canaan, for an everlasting possession; and I will be their God." (Genesis 17:8)

In time, everything will pass away:

"Heaven and earth shall pass away, but my words shall not pass away." (Matthew 24:35)

The only thing everlasting is God and His word. Jesus is, and always was, the promise spoken forth by God! He was the promised Seed, and the inheritance the prophets before Him sought after:

"By faith he sojourned in the land of promise, as in a strange country, dwelling in tabernacles with Isaac and Jacob, the heirs with him of the same promise: For he looked for a city which hath foundations, whose builder and maker is God…they wandered in deserts, and in mountains, and in dens and caves of the earth. And these all, having obtained a good report through faith, received not the promise." Hebrews 11:9-10, 38-39

When Jesus came to the earth, He told His disciples:

"For I tell you, that many prophets and kings have desired to see those things which ye see, and have not seen them; and to hear those things which ye hear, and have not heard them." (Luke 10:24)

Whether the world knows it or not, they are seeking a treasure that is only found in Christ.

25 Years

"By faith Abraham, when he was called to go out into a place which he should after receive for an inheritance, obeyed; and he went out, not knowing whither he went." (Hebrews 11:8)

Often, we read through a story of a Bible character within a few minutes, and fail to consider the lifetime it took to complete. We see the promise spoken by God, and within a few pages turned, we witness their desired end. However, what's unwritten are the decades of patient surrender.

Let's take a moment and speak on the patriarch's faith. Consider Abraham and the promise declared.

At 75 years old, the Lord called Abram out of his father's house and country and foretold of the nations that would be birthed through him.

At 76 years old, nothing had changed; the promise hadn't changed, nor was it yet delivered.

The Lord continued to speak forth His promise to Abraham and reminded him that his seed would be more numerable than the dust of the earth, than the stars in the sky, and how he would inherit the land of promise, *yet* his wife was barren! Don't you think the Lord knew it was impossible before He called you to do it? The pre-requisite of a miracle is an impossibility.

Another year passed: Abraham turned 77. Nothing had changed; the promise hadn't changed, nor was it yet delivered.

Every day for the next year, Abraham and Sarah rose early in the morning and laid their heads down at night, childless. Abraham turned 78.

Three more years passed: Abraham turned 81. Abraham's body was getting older, and Sarah's womb, barren still.

Five more years passed.

As time progressed, all they could hold on to is what the Lord spoke. There wasn't anything seen to prove what God had spoken would come to pass. Abraham didn't have any natural hope:

"(As it is written, I have made thee a father of many nations,) before him whom he believed, even God, who quickeneth the dead, and calleth those things which be not as though they were. Who against hope believed in hope, that he might become the father of many nations, according to that which was spoken, So shall thy seed be." (Romans 4:17, 18)

If you were promised rain, and consistently gazed upon a light blue and cloudless sky for months on end, you would more than likely lose all hope. However, if you were promised rain after months of drought, and the once cloudless sky formed a small and dark rolling cloud... that small cloud would've become your great hope! Nevertheless, this is an example of natural hope. Biblical hope is not based on what is seen:

"For we are saved by hope: but hope that is seen is not hope: for what a man seeth, why doth he yet hope for?" (Romans 8:24)

If we are comparing Abraham's situation to this example, his would be that of a cloudless and light blue sky for 25 years. In the natural, he and his wife's bodies were hopeless. For this reason, the Lord gave them His word to hope in, not their bodies.

He said: *"look at the sand, look at the stars."*

When they found themselves looking down, behold, the promise in the sand. Looking up at the stars when things got dark, confirmed what God initially declared. The sand on the shore and the stars in the sky were written for our admonition. This was Abraham and Sarah's way of meditating on His word.

God was telling Abraham to take his eyes off the circumstance and fix them on the promise. In like manner, we cannot look to the present to determine our future, but only what God has promised in the abundance of His word.

It may not rain every day, but the sand and the stars are constant. We need to prepare our field before the rain, not during the rain. That's faith. When there's not a cloud in the sky, and you're building an ark... we need to be like Noah.

(Imagine how much easier it would have been for Abraham and Sarah to believe God's word if their bodies became younger and livelier, with each year that passed. Had that been the case, it would have been much simpler for them to believe God's promise! However, this was not the case. Their bodies did not seem to line up with the promise God declared.

Similarly, with us, we receive a promise from God, but our circumstances don't seem to reflect what God spoke; they seem to be going in the other direction! It would be easy for us to believe God when everything in the natural lines up, but the natural things often contradict the things of the spirit, and vice versa. To experience God's promises in the physical realm, we must first see them in the spiritual realm. We cannot rely on what we see with our eyes, but what we see with the eyes of our heart. It may not be easy, but it is the only way.)

At this point, Abraham was 86. Sarah persuaded Abraham to lie with her Egyptian maid to produce an heir. We don't seem to find much of a resistance from him in scripture! Abraham obeyed his wife! This was written for our admonition as well: *Taking our eyes off the sand and stars will give birth to something from Egypt.*

It is of the utmost importance to take God at His word and to not make provision for the flesh. We inherit the promises through faith and patience, not lust and haste.

Nevertheless, before Ishmael, Abraham believed God and it was accounted to him for righteousness. Later, when Isaac was born, the Lord said, *"Take your only son with you..."* (Genesis 22:2). Have you ever questioned:

"What about Ishmael?"

When we are washed in the blood of Jesus and have been made righteous, God doesn't see our past. He only sees Isaac (Jesus).

God spoke a promise to us, and we can only look to Him for its completion. We may be barren for a season, but the Lord alone opens the womb.

God may have given you a vision of a successful business, but your bank account says otherwise. The Lord may have said you'd be speaking in front of millions of people, yet you struggle with your words. (Funny, Moses said the same thing.) You may have been told by God that you'd bring restoration to broken families, yet you're divorced, and your kids aren't living at home. God calls those things that be not as though they were.

It has been said if you can carry out the vision God has given you on your own, it probably wasn't Him to begin with. All three of the patriarchs had barren wives; signifying, the promise declared can only be accomplished by God Himself.

Take courage, take your eyes off the circumstance, and trust God with all your heart. Steadfast hope is the anchor of your soul, not the way you feel. If Abraham looked to his circumstance to determine his future, he wouldn't have one.

...87

Abraham and his wife were now one year older and one year closer to seemingly nothing at all. Twelve years have passed since the promise was spoken. Twelve years with no end in sight.

Another three years passed; Abraham turned 90. We're privileged to know from hindsight, but he nor his wife knew there were still another ten years to go! Thank God for His mercy in coming to us at 99 and saying you will have the son in the next year. We can bear one more year after we have just borne 24! It is certainly easier to look back at the time passed than to dwell on the long road ahead, but we must take one step at a time, nonetheless.

"Better is the end of a thing than the beginning thereof: and the patient in spirit is better than the proud in spirit." (Ecclesiastes 7:8)

At 99 years old, the Lord appeared to Abram, changed his name to Abraham, and his wife's name to Sarah, and spoke once again of the promise He made and declared that Sarah would bear a child the following year.

*"And the LORD visited Sarah **as he had said**, and the LORD did unto Sarah **as he had spoken**. For Sarah conceived, and bare Abraham a son in his old age, **at the set time** of which God had spoken to him." (Genesis 21:1-2) (emphasis mine)*

"A woman when she is in travail hath sorrow, because her hour is come: but as soon as she is delivered of the child, she remembereth no more the anguish, for joy that a man is born into the world." (John 16:21)

From conception to delivery, the process is hidden. We can't see what's being formed or what is truly taking place. Nevertheless, our faith is being formed through the process of hope. It won't be premature, nor will it be late. "...At this set time in the next year... at the set time of which God had spoken to him" (Genesis 17:21, 21:2). God has a set time. When the baby is born, you forget the time and sorrow, and you rejoice in the laughter of the promise.

Abraham and Sarah patiently waited for the promise God had spoken to come to pass. Isaac was symbolic of the promise the whole earth patiently waited for; that promise was Christ.

What we will touch on next will paint another portrait of the Christ Who would come, through the observance of Abib.

Abib

The book of Malachi separates the New Testament from the Old by four hundred silent years. Jesus' birth also separated two eras of time as we know it on earth: B.C.: *Before Christ*, and A.D.: *Anno Domini*: which is Latin, meaning: *in the year of our Lord*. Jesus' birth changed everything as we know it, including time!

Not to say that time ceased or stopped and started again, but how we revolve our calendar years around the birth of our Lord Jesus Christ. It is safe to say that the world revolves around Jesus! In fact, it was all made and is held together by the word (Hebrews 1:3, Colossians 1:17, John 1:3), which *is* Jesus (John 1:1-5, 14).

Contrary to popular belief, or unbelief rather, we have not been around for millions of years. Not only do the calendar years for man account for 6,000 years, but the genesis of the earth itself equates to 6,000 years. (Now, this chapter's goal is not to prove a young earth, but rather bring to light significant timeframes in the Bible and how they correlate to us today through Christ. For this reason, I will not delve deep into this subject. I highly recommend reading *"The Waters Cleaved,"* by Dr. Grady McMurtry, for an in-depth study of creation to prove this point further.)

With that said, consider this new beginning:

"And the LORD spake unto Moses and Aaron in the land of Egypt, saying, This month [Abib] shall be unto you the beginning of months: it shall be the first month of the year to you." (Exodus 12:1, 2) (brackets mine)

The month Abib, which means: *an ear of corn, the month of newly ripened grain*, would become the first month to begin the new year. This is extremely significant! The beginning of the Jewish new year changed based on the night of the Passover.

Abib is a stage of barley growth and harvest, rather than a definitive month start. For example, January 1st, February 1st, March 1st, etc., will occur based on our set solar year. We're basically on a countdown from 365 to 0. The Jewish people are on a solar schedule for the year itself, but a lunar schedule for the determination of their months. In comparison, our monthly calendars are much different.

The way they determine the start of their new year is based on the timeframe of Abib (between April and May) and the new moon. They need to look up towards heaven for direction before they set their schedules on earth.

So, why the change in observance? Why would the Lord have a new beginning for the year based on observing Abib? I will give you a hint: it has everything to do with Jesus being the observance, (whether the Jewish people yet believe that or not).

Before we go any further, consider the creation of the heavenly lights and their purpose:

*"And God said, Let there be lights in the firmament of the heaven to divide the day from the night; **and let them be for signs**, and for seasons, and for days, and years." (Genesis 1:14) (emphasis mine)*

Isn't it interesting how the Lord spoke "let there be light" before He made the sun? He hadn't yet made the sun, the moon, or the stars, but there was already light from His spoken word on day one. The lights in the firmament were created on day four!

This is significant because in Revelation it says:

"And there shall be no night there; and they need no candle, neither light of the sun; for the Lord God giveth them light: and they shall reign for ever and ever." (Revelation 22:5)

Which means, our source has always been Jesus. Even more important than the sun for our existence on earth is our dependency on the light of His word for our sustenance. If that's not a sign that points to Jesus, what is?

Besides dividing the day and night, these lights were created first for signs. The most important sign yet was the star of Bethlehem in the east over the newly birthed Messiah (Matthew 2:1-2). There have been signs since, and there will be more to come; but for now, let's get back to Abib.

The Broken Barley

If we are considering *what* the Lord is having the children of Israel observe in this new year beginning for them, it is this: the *way* He saved them in the first place. The whole Exodus was a foreshadow of the deliverance to come through Jesus. Every plague was purposed leading up to the night of the Passover.

One of the judgments brought upon the land of Egypt was hail mixed with fire:

"So there was hail, and fire mingled with the hail, very grievous, such as there was none like it in all the land of Egypt since it became a nation. And the hail smote throughout all the land of Egypt all that was in the field, both man and beast; and the hail smote every herb of the field, and brake every tree of the field. Only in the land of Goshen, where the children of Israel were, was there no hail." (Exodus 9:24-26)

Every tree in Egypt broke due to the severity of this hailstorm! What also caught my attention in this passage aligned with a later verse. It is Abib's definition:

"And the flax and the barley was smitten: for the barley was in the ear, and the flax was bolled." (Exodus 9:31)

Barley is sown at the end of winter and is harvested as a firstfruit of spring. Interestingly, the newly ripened grain was destroyed by the plague of the Lord. Keep this prior passage in mind as we elaborate on the first Passover, and how it was eaten:

"And thus shall ye eat it; with your loins girded, your shoes on your feet, and your staff in your hand; and ye shall eat it in haste: it is the LORD's passover. For I will pass through the land of Egypt this night, and will smite all the firstborn in the land of Egypt, both man and beast; and against all the gods of Egypt I will execute judgment: I am the LORD." (Exodus 12:11, 12)

With the account of the first Passover and its administration being mentioned, let's now touch on the substance of this foreshadow through the feeding of the five thousand, and tie it all together:

"There is a lad here, which hath five barley loaves..." (John 6:9)

"And he commanded them to make all sit down by companies upon the green grass. And they sat down in ranks, by hundreds, and by fifties. And when he had taken the five loaves and the two fishes, he looked up to heaven, and blessed, and brake the loaves, and gave them to his disciples to set before them; and the two fishes divided he among them all." (Mark 6:39-41)

The first Passover was eaten in haste. They ate with their sandals on and their staffs in their hands. They also ate the lamb with bitter herbs. This meal was not intended to be enjoyed! However, when Jesus knew Passover was approaching, He told His disciples to make the men *sit* down in the grass. Jesus, the Passover Lamb, fed them in rest!

In the first Passover, each family killed a lamb and fed from it, but Jesus, the one Lamb, fed them! There must have been thousands of sheep that were slaughtered in the first Passover, but when Jesus came, He testified how He would be the one Lamb that would feed all. How did He feed them? He blessed and broke the barley loaves.

The barley was smitten.

Jesus testified how He would be the newly ripened grain offering that was smitten by the judgment of God on our behalf. He was broken, so we could be blessed.

"And the flax and the barley was smitten: for the barley was in the ear, and the flax was bolled. But the wheat and the rie were not smitten: for they were not grown up." (Exodus 9:31, 32)

The barley was struck, so we could be spared. Thank you, Jesus!

What can also be gleaned is how Jesus was taken early. He was killed at 33 years old. He wasn't a child, nor yet an old man.

"Then said the Jews unto him, Thou art not yet 50 years old, and hast thou seen Abraham?" (John 8:57)

Jesus wasn't afforded a long life here on the earth. At Calvary, He ate of the bitter herbs for us while standing so we could be at rest. He was "cut off out of the land of the living" (Isaiah 53:8). He didn't belong here (as far as being earthly) as much as sin and sickness didn't belong on His body.

"...My kingdom is not of this world..." (John 18:36)

There wasn't even room for the King of Glory at the inn. He was born amongst animals and placed in a manger. Later, shepherds came to visit Him. He was the ram caught in the thicket, the promised Lamb of God. He wasn't born in comfort; He was born to die.

> *"For he shall grow up before him as a tender plant, and as a root out of a dry ground..." (Isaiah 53:2)*

He didn't come to root Himself deep on earth; He came here to transplant Himself within us.

> *"Yet it pleased the LORD to bruise him; he hath put him to grief: when thou shalt make his soul an offering for sin, he shall see his seed, he shall prolong his days, and the pleasure of the LORD shall prosper in his hand." (Isaiah 53:10)*

We are His seed, and He shall prolong His days on the earth through us, His body.

Jesus would also fulfill the *way* the first Passover was eaten. They ate the lamb quickly with their staffs in their hands. The staff that Jesus held in His hands while making His way to Calvary was the cross.

Furthermore, the symbolism of their loins being girded about with sandals on their feet signified how they were ready to journey. Jesus wasn't going to stay on the cross. He's alive and well! The cross was not His final destination: we were.

430/430

> *"And he said unto Abram, Know of a surety that thy seed shall be a stranger in a land that is not theirs, and shall serve them; and they shall afflict them four hundred years." Genesis 15:13*

There is another timeframe that correlates well with the fulfillment of Jesus' life. I had mentioned it prior concerning the four hundred silent years. This era of silence separated the New Covenant and the Old, between Malachi and the Gospels.

During that time, there wasn't any move of God recorded, nor any prophet speaking on His behalf. Significantly, there were four hundred years of enslavement and four hundred years of silence. Concerning the chronology of Moses delivering the Israelites and Jesus beginning His ministry, we can see there was no coincidence.

In Genesis, the Lord foretold Abraham how his seed would be enslaved and that afterward, He would deliver them. The deliverer He raised up was Moses.

> *"Now the sojourning of the children of Israel, who dwelt in Egypt,* **was four hundred and thirty years**. *And it came to pass at the end of the four hundred and thirty years, even the selfsame day it came to pass, that all the hosts of the LORD went out from the land of Egypt. It* is *a night to be much observed unto the LORD for bringing them out from the land of Egypt: this* is *that night of the LORD to be observed of all the children of Israel in their generations." (Exodus 12:40-42) (emphasis mine)*

Consider the comparison of events: The children of Israel dwelt in Egypt for 430 years, then the Lord raised up Moses to deliver them. On the night of the Passover, they went through the Red Sea as a form of baptism and then entered the wilderness. 430 years.

There were 400 silent years before Christ.

The Lord then raised up the true deliverer: Jesus. He was baptized in the Jordan River at 30 years old, and then went straight into the wilderness. 430 years!

430 years in the Old Testament, 430 years in the New.

Not only did Jesus fulfill all prophecy concerning Himself, but He also fulfilled the whole picture.

During the children of Israel's stay in the wilderness, they responded to temptation with murmurings and complaints. During Jesus' short stay in the wilderness, He responded to temptation by the word.

Jesus spent 40 *days* in the wilderness; the Israelites spent 40 *years*.

> *"And your children shall wander in the wilderness forty years, and bear your whoredoms, until your carcases be wasted in the wilderness. After the number of the days in which ye searched the land, even forty days, each day for a year, shall ye bear your iniquities, even forty years, and ye shall know my breach of promise." (Numbers 14:33, 34)*

The children of Israel spent a year for every day the spies dwelt in the promised land, because they believed their report over God's.

Following Jesus' example, we find the Lord only had a short season in mind for the children of Israel in the desert. We see a contrast between Jesus and the Israelites in scripture. Whose example will you choose?

Chapter Three

Out Of Egypt

"I have a past, but I don't live there anymore."

In this chapter, we'll go in-depth into the importance of not looking back to where we came from. We'll see that looking back and not looking unto Jesus, causes most of our trouble in the first place. We'll also discuss a misconception that's held most of the body of Christ in captivity.

As mentioned in the first chapter, we began our journey on the mountain top. We will now go down to Red Sea level to see what occurs at redemption.

Coming "out of Egypt" is where we leave behind our old man, reckon him dead, and put on Christ. This is where we journey to a place we've never been before. Like Abraham, it is where we leave the house of our father, and trust a God we've never served before. We leave our idols behind, along with our past lives floating dead on the seashore.

It is the time of leaving the leaven of Egypt behind. It is not the time to linger or second guess, but the time to journey forward. It is our exodus; it is our new beginning.

Passover

"...spoken of the Lord by the prophet, saying, Out of Egypt have I called my son." (Matthew 2:15)

We gain everything we'll ever need upon our exodus out of Egypt. Because of the Passover, we come out with jewels, divine health, new clothing, and best of all: a brand-new nature. We come out in what's called *shalom*, which is: *God's peace*: which is summed up in this English word: *whole*.

This is a wonderful depiction of our salvation. We relate to the children of Israel today because our salvation mirrors that of Israel being delivered out of Egypt.

Pharaoh, who despised Joseph's legacy, made the lives of the Israelites harsh and bitter. Through generations of enslavement, and weariness of life, he wanted to destroy the most valuable thing of all: hope. He would have been successful had the Lord not intervened.

This is also true today: had the Lord not intervened through Jesus coming to earth and dying for us, there would have been no way out; we would have been trapped forever in generational enslavement by the devil. Just like the children of Israel were born into slavery in Egypt, we were born in sin. We were destined for hell, *but* Jesus paid the price for our salvation. He was our only way out!

We have all been delivered out of Egypt when we made Jesus the Lord of our life. It is only through His ransom that we can be saved. His Life for ours.

Pharaoh ensured that there was no way for the children of Israel to save themselves. They were going to need a deliverer whether they knew it or not. We all need a Moses to come and tell us the plan and way out (Exodus 4:29-31). He was a type of Christ in this portion of history because he was the deliverer that the Lord raised up, and the prophet that spoke of the Prophet to come:

"The LORD thy God will raise up unto thee a Prophet from the midst of thee, of thy brethren, like unto me; unto him ye shall hearken." (Deuteronomy 18:15)

After Moses proved to the Israelites how the Lord had sent him, ten plagues were performed upon Egypt. The last plague particularly, was the death of all the firstborn males. The death angel passed over the homes of the Israelite's who painted their doorposts with blood. The Lord was painting a picture: The blood of Christ would be the key that opened the door of salvation for all who would enter.

"Then said Jesus unto them again, Verily, verily, I say unto you, I am the door of the sheep." (John 10:7)

Jesus reminds us there is only *one* way:

"Jesus saith unto him, I am the way, the truth, and the life: no man cometh unto the Father, but by me." (John 14:6)

The death angel visited every house in Egypt. Only those who went through the way instructed were spared. Even if a Jew were found without the blood on the doorpost, his firstborn would've been killed like everyone else's. Death will pass over us all, and at the end of our lives, if we are not found to have gone through the bloody Door, we will not be spared. This Door is Jesus.

The Bible says there was a mixed multitude that exited Egypt along with the Israelite's. This means they walked through the Door and adhered to the Passover as well.

"And a mixed multitude went up also with them; and flocks, and herds, even very much cattle." (Exodus 12:38)

Various cultures went out from Egypt to enter the promised land. The Lord intended salvation to be for all. Notice what God said about a stranger who would commit to the Passover:

"And when a stranger shall sojourn with thee, and will keep the passover to the LORD, let all his males be circumcised, and then let him come near and keep it; and he shall be as one that is born in the land: for no uncircumcised person shall eat thereof. One law shall be to him that is homeborn, and unto the stranger that sojourneth among you." (Exodus 12:48, 49)

Whether a born Jew or born gentile becomes *born-again*, we all become one in Christ Jesus:

"But he is a Jew, which is one inwardly; and circumcision is that of the heart, in the spirit, and not in the letter; whose praise is not of men, but of God." (Romans 2:29)

We were never afterthoughts of God. We were on His mind well before the heavens, or the earth was created. Whether a born Jew or born Gentile: we were *all* born in Egypt with a false identity. The baptism through the Red Sea would cut off the umbilical cord of Egypt.

Red Sea Baptism

> *"Moreover, brethren, I would not that ye should be ignorant, how that all our fathers were under the cloud, and all passed through the sea; And were all baptized unto Moses in the cloud and in the sea; And did all eat the same spiritual meat; And did all drink the same spiritual drink: for they drank of that spiritual Rock that followed them: and that Rock was Christ." (1ˢᵗ Corinthians 10:1-4)*

This significant account was written to show what transpired at the Red Sea, and how it mirrors our baptism into Christ.

> *"And it was told the king of Egypt that the people fled: and the heart of Pharaoh and of his servants was turned against the people, and they said, Why have we done this, that we have let Israel go from serving us?...And the LORD hardened the heart of Pharaoh king of Egypt, and he pursued after the children of Israel: and the children of Israel went out with an high hand." (Exodus 14:5, 8)*

When the enemy realizes that we've been redeemed by the blood of the Lamb and have made our way out of the world to serve the Lord, it is then when he doesn't want to let us go. He tries to overtake us, and bring us back into bondage to serve him. As we read further, we see how the Lord used the water to cut off Pharaoh and his army from pursuit.

> *"And the LORD said unto Moses, Stretch out thine hand over the sea, that the waters may come again upon the Egyptians, upon their chariots, and upon their horsemen... Thus the LORD saved Israel that day out of the hand of the Egyptians; and Israel saw the Egyptians dead upon the sea shore. And Israel saw that great work which the LORD did upon the Egyptians: and the people feared the LORD, and believed the LORD, and his servant Moses." (Exodus 14:26, 30-31)*

When we are born-again, we must be baptized as a symbolism of what the Lord did through Jesus Christ on our behalf. What did He do? He died on the cross (the firstborn Son); Became the bloody Door to walk through (our Passover); Was buried and spent three days in hell (three-day journey to the waters of Marrah); Then resurrected from the dead three days later (waters made sweet).

*"Thy right hand, O LORD, is become glorious in power: thy right hand,
O LORD, hath dashed in pieces the enemy." (Exodus 15:6)*

The Father's Right Hand (Jesus) has made a way for us!

The Lord used the water to cut off our old life. There is no way back to the
Egypt we once knew. To even return to Egypt, we would have to swim back
through the Red Sea, only to find a land destroyed. Not to mention, when the
river and land were at its best, we were enslaved.

We have been given a brand-new nature through baptism!

*"For ye are all the children of God by faith in Christ Jesus. For as many
of you as have been baptized into Christ have put on Christ." (Galatians
3:26, 27)*

We have been translated into a brand-new kingdom!

*"Who hath delivered us from the power of darkness, and hath translated
us into the kingdom of his dear Son." (Colossians 1:13)*

New nature, new kingdom, new King.

In light of this, I would like to strongly emphasize how we are not merely
sinners saved by grace, but the righteousness of God in Christ Jesus.

*"For every one that useth milk is unskilful in the **word of righteousness**:
for he is a babe. But strong meat belongeth to them that are of full age,
even those who by reason of use have their senses exercised to discern
both good and evil." (Hebrews 5:13, 14) (emphasis mine)*

The word of righteousness is the meat of God's word! It is time for us to
embrace the finished work of Jesus, agree with who He says we are, and walk
in our new identity.

Know Ye Not?

As this book pertains to what transpired at the Exodus, it's important to
discuss what truly happened. That is, we have three parts to our being: spirit,
soul and body (1st Thessalonians 5:23). In relation to this book, it is in that
same order: Out of Egypt (spirit); The wilderness (soul); The promised land
(body).

Though exiting Egypt was a symbolism of death to our old man, we were
given life and a brand-new *spirit*. Beauty for ashes.

The wilderness process is the ongoing renewal of our *soul* in Christ through the mirror of His word.

The promised land is walking out the fullness of our inheritance in the *body*.

The promised land pertains to spiritual maturity, physical healing, and monetary gain as well. The Lord desires for all that occurred within the spiritual realm to translate into the physical. Understanding this process will place a great value on the wilderness.

We enter the wilderness after Passover in shalom; we come out of Egypt whole. Our born-again spirits will not become more holy or more "born-again" than they are at this very moment. It all comes together when we understand we've been made brand-new in our spirit, and then *sealed* by the Holy Spirit (Ephesians 1:13). We have everything we'll ever need in our perfected spirit! We have the same spirit now that we'll have in heaven!

> *"For by one offering he hath perfected for ever them that are sanctified."* (Hebrews 10:14)

To validate with an Old Testament verse of what occurs at salvation:

> *"A new heart also will I give you, and a new spirit will I put within you: and I will take away the stony heart out of your flesh, and I will give you an heart of flesh." (Ezekiel 36:26)*

This new spirit is now the new you. We've been granted a new heart for God's ways to be written upon.

> *"But this shall be the covenant that I will make with the house of Israel; After those days, saith the LORD, I will put my law in their inward parts, and write it in their hearts; and will be their God, and they shall be my people." (Jeremiah 31:33)*

Mirror/Mirror

Regarding our new nature, let's clarify any possible misconceptions about the perfection that occurred within.

When first looking in the mirror and appearing the same, we may question where we've been perfected. However, we cannot look in the natural to determine who we are. We must only look to the mirror of God's word for our true reflection. The word reveals that which has *already* occurred within; the word reveals the hidden man of the heart. To see ourselves, we must see Him.

*"And the two disciples **heard him speak**, and they followed Jesus. Then Jesus turned, and saw them following, and saith unto them, **What seek ye?** They said unto him, Rabbi, (which is to say, being interpreted, Master,) **where dwellest thou?** He saith unto them, Come and see..."* (John 1:37-39) (emphasis mine)

Jesus dwells in His word and He is now within us! The disciples heard him speak and were told, "come and see." Following Jesus in where He lives is to seek Him out in His word. This mirror speaks!

If not within, where else do you think Jesus perfected you? It is certainly not in the physical. How else do you think you're entering heaven? This is vital to understand because most believers are walking around condemned, and some are even unsure of their salvation altogether. Truly, it is understanding righteousness that makes us confident towards God.

See, we come out of Egypt righteous. It's what has already occurred within. It's not something attained in the promised land, it's given from the start through the Passover; through the blood of the Lamb on the door.

Understanding righteousness will keep us free from condemnation, and grant us boldness towards God:

"Beloved, if our heart condemn us not, then have we confidence toward God." (1ˢᵗ John 3:21)

The verse before this says if our heart condemns us, God is greater than our heart. In other words, God wants us to have confidence in Him even if our heart seems to be conflicted. We may agree with the accuser of the brethren, and we may allow others to condemn us; our own heart may fail us, and we may even condemn ourselves, but it is never God.

We need to run confidently to His throne of grace to obtain mercy in our time of need. Jesus is our grace! Running *to* Jesus and not *from* Him, will expose our struggle to His light and empower us to live holy. It is in the times of uncertainty that we need to trust Him even more, despite how we may feel.

We may *feel* like running away, but this is our soul trying to maintain control. The more we run to Him for mercy in times of trouble, the more we find ourselves creating a healthy reliance on His grace. A true understanding of grace will empower you to deny the lusts of the flesh, rather than feed them in the first place. Grace will show you the way out, not "cover" your sin.

We do not sin, and then say: *"Well, I'm covered by His grace."*

This would be an error. The grace of God does not merely cover your sin. It is the unmerited favor that empowers you to walk in true holiness.

Pertaining to our continuous walk with God, the enemy has tricked us into thinking grace was taboo:

"Sure, we understand that God saved us by His grace, but we mustn't have too much of it. Certainly, too much grace will cause us to do whatever we want..."

My friends, this is a lie of the enemy altogether. For one, you can never have too much grace. In each of Paul's epistles, he would address in his salutation, "grace and peace be unto you!" Peter said, "grace and peace be *multiplied* to you," in both of his!

Secondly, the way we have defined grace has been wrong. We have been told that grace was something granted to us when we sin:

"Oh, well, there's grace for that."

The "grace for that" will empower you to deny the sin altogether! When we realize that grace is not a message, but a Man (Jesus), we soon discover that a healthy reliance on grace will empower us to truly change.

Someone who has a true revelation of God's grace will not desire to continue in sin. Their walk with Christ is one of intimacy, not infidelity. It is one of openness, not secrecy. To this individual, they will not desire to see how much they can get away with, but rather to discover the depths of His love.

Consider this: Adam and Eve hid in the garden amongst the trees after sinning. Why? Because they were afraid of God and of the condemnation to come. They covered their nakedness with fig leaves. The Lord then covered them with coats of skins, signifying the sacrifice to come.

We must realize we are *already* hidden in Christ because of the Last Adam (Colossians 3:3). We might as well run to Him, not away. There is nowhere to hide but in Him.

"Neither is there any creature that is not manifest in his sight: but all things are naked and opened unto the eyes of him with whom we have to do." (Hebrews 4:13)

So, run to Him, not from Him, in time of trouble. It's not the throne of condemnation, it is the throne of grace. He is looking to save us, not throw stones.

He Who Has An Ear

"For a just man falleth seven times, and riseth up again: but the wicked shall fall into mischief." (Proverbs 24:16)

Agreeing with what the Lord has already finished on the cross, and declaring His promises over our lives, will fan the holy fire within. We ought to confess: *"I am the righteousness of God in Christ; I am the head and not the tail; I'm above only, and not beneath; I am loved by my Father!"*, every time we look in the mirror. In fact, we should confess this *especially* when we don't feel like it! We need to hear this daily, because this is how faith comes.

*"But the **righteousness** which is of faith **speaketh**..." (Romans 10:6) (emphasis mine)*

Instead of struggling to change our behavior, we should declare what the word says about us. This, in turn, allows Jesus to change our desires. This focus on righteousness and grace will empower Jesus to take control and change us from the inside out.

Some of us confess all the sins we've committed that night before we go to sleep and even ask forgiveness for the ones we can't recall. Some born-again, Spirit-filled Christians, re-dedicate their lives to Jesus at the altar on a monthly basis. This isn't the milk of God's word, it's the condemnation of the devil! They don't know who they truly are.

In this frustrating cycle, some believe they are just one sin away from disappointing the Lord. Erroneous doctrine will have some believing they are in Christian AA meetings, saying: *"Hi, I'm David, and I'm just a sinner saved by grace."*

This mentality encourages people to believe they are always one sin away from losing fellowship with God. This is not true. The Holy Spirit is not condemning us of who we once were, He reminds us of who we are now in Christ.

This is how we can begin to distinguish the voice of God from the voice of the devil. When we hear: *"Again? You're not over this by now? How do you expect to lead others to me when you can't take the lead over yourself? How many times have we gone through this? How can you pray for others now? They won't be healed... remember what you did the other day?"*

This, my beloved brethren is the voice of the accuser of the brethren, and we need to disregard this completely. This is not the voice of the Shephard. If we fall, the Holy Spirit points us to Christ:

"Son, this is not who you are. You have been purchased with a price. You are holy (Hebrews 3:1). You are righteous (Romans 10:10). You are saved and sanctified. You are just like Jesus! (1 John 4:17). This may be what you did... but this is not who you are."

When we listen to the accuser and not the Holy Spirit, we condemn ourselves and pay some type of penance in our hearts. We sit and sulk over what we have done for hours, or even days at a time. The Lord doesn't want us living on a roller coaster. He wants us to live in peace.

I know this all too well because this was me.

I knew I was saved, and there was no doubt God loved me. He became my Father and my reason for living! He filled me with a love like I had never experienced before, and He gave me purpose.

When the scales fell from my eyes, the sky became bluer and the grass became greener! I recall being struck by the sheer majesty of God's creation. I was enthralled at the beauty of the trees and the flowers and thought:

"Is this what they've looked like all along?"

I was living in a brand-new world! I was completely changed; I was truly born-again! Despite this wonderful new reality, I was feeding on a legalistic diet. My new nature was rarely the focus when being ministered unto, but mostly the old. Little did I know, my growth was being stunted.

The problem occurs from the little leaven that spoils the whole lump. A little poison takes a toll on you at the end, but with one bite at a time, you won't necessarily notice it.

Leaven Of Hypocrisy

Jesus warned us:

*"...Beware ye of the leaven of the Pharisees, which is **hypocrisy.**" (Luke 12:1) (emphasis mine)*

He likened it unto yeast that rises in bread. We are to eat from the Bread of Life and have Him alone rise in our hearts.

Religious leaven is behavior modification rather than true inward change. We cannot clean up the outside while our soul is left untouched within. Look at what Jesus has to say about this approach:

"Woe unto you, scribes and Pharisees, hypocrites! for ye make clean the outside of the cup and of the platter, but within they are full of extortion and excess. Thou blind Pharisee, cleanse first that which is within the cup and platter, that the outside of them may be clean also." (Matthew 23:25, 26)

Real change can never occur from a focus on the outer. This is hypocrisy. Real change can only occur from Jesus within.

Hypocrisy is putting on the facade of "looking the part," but inside your soul, you are merely keeping the lusts of the flesh at bay.

Here are some of the signs you've been feeding off the Pharisee's leaven:

You have a victim mentality and believe that sin is out to get you.

You're trying your best not to sin, but you're paranoid that around every corner is your eventual downfall.

Subconsciously, you believe that you're only as good as your last prayer, or your last spiritual accomplishment.

Your intentions are always good, but you hardly seem to meet them.

You smile at church, but you know that when you get home, you're going to give in to your unchanged mind and fall.

You don't know how to escape...

You have a desire to live victoriously, but you are struggling with the same sins that have beset you in Egypt. This has been the enemy's tactic all along: eventually admit you are a hypocrite and completely backslide; walk away from God and throw in the towel.

"Even so ye also outwardly appear righteous unto men, but within ye are full of hypocrisy and iniquity." (Matthew 23:28)

Trying to appear righteous won't work. In our hearts, we know that we cannot fool God, yet we frustrate ourselves because we can't seem to change! Take courage. You are not the problem. You already have everything you'll ever need within. A change in perspective is all that's necessary.

My brothers and sisters, be encouraged if this is, or once was you; because it's not you... it's your diet. This leaven has crippled the body of Christ. Not intentionally, and not by choice, but we have frustrated the grace of God through the constant digestion of law-based ministry. For this cause, Jesus told us to beware.

We must understand this: the law was not created for a righteous man (1 Timothy 1:9). The law will always expose you as a hypocrite:

"For that which I do I allow not: for what I would, that do I not; but what I hate, that do I." (Romans 7:15)

The law will cause you to *do* what you hate, and *not do* the good you've intended. For this reason, we must let grace become our teacher (Titus 2:11, 12); which is not a tablet of stone, but a man who came in the flesh: Jesus!

"For the law was given by Moses, but grace and truth came by Jesus Christ." (John 1:17)

If you believe you need to "catch up to Jesus," you'll always fall behind the curve; but through the realization that you're starting at the finish line with Christ and going forward, you'll only succeed.

Through immersing our souls in the true gospel, the outside of our cup will be cleansed by default.

The leaven of the Pharisees is countered by surrendering to His grace. Through humbly accepting the gift of righteousness, and focusing on the risen Christ, you will start to see a lasting change without even trying. Then, grace will be grace.

An apple tree doesn't struggle to produce fruit. It births forth an apple naturally. Focus on the root and the fruit will take care of itself.

A healthy perspective of who God is and what His grace accomplishes will grant us unfettered access to walk in the garden once more with Him. In my Biblical opinion, the true definition of righteousness is the *right* to stand with God through Christ. The redeemed ability to walk with God again. Amen.

Regarding the gift of righteousness given, let's discuss what else was granted when leaving Egypt. The spoiling of the Egyptians will shed some light on God's good nature.

Spoiled

"But every woman shall borrow of her neighbor, and of her that sojourneth in her house, jewels of silver, and jewels of gold, and raiment: and ye shall put them upon your sons, and upon your daughters; and ye shall spoil the Egyptians." (Exodus 3:22)

Upon reading this account, I noticed the manner the children of Israel exited Egypt:

"And also that nation, whom they shall serve, will I judge: and afterward shall they come out with great substance." (Genesis 15:14)

See, the Israelites were slaves in Egypt. They were told when to eat and when to work. Ultimately, they were told how to live... which wasn't living at all. Their portion was bitterness and poverty prior to their deliverance.

They then came out of Egypt with great wealth... but made their way right into the desert! Where would they spend it all in the first place? Truly, this was all part of God's plan. They may have come out with riches but weren't mature enough to handle the responsibility of it.

In Exodus 32, they demanded that Aaron make them an idol due to their disregard and impatience. If patience is not properly perfected within our hearts, we'll soon find ourselves fashioning a golden calf with the gold we took from Egypt. We will spend our time and money for evil if we don't allow the Lord to sanctify us first.

We must first be sanctified and set apart, and then what's placed in our hands will be used for good.

Money is neither good nor bad. It is amoral. The *love* of money is the root of all evil (1st Timothy 6:10). We know this: we cannot serve God and money. Jesus calls it a master. The Lord wants to slay the master of money in our lives, so we're not forging deaf idols with our golden earrings; it's to be set aside for the building of God's tabernacle.

"An inheritance may be gotten hastily at the beginning; but the end thereof shall not be blessed." (Proverbs 20:21)

No one would hand a toddler the keys to their car and expect them to drive. They would quickly place the keys right into their mouths. Also, (without proper instruction), we wouldn't simply hand over the keys to our teenager and say: "Go have fun!" They would soon crash. One day, we have in mind to bless them with the keys and the car, but not before the time.

If sent into the world without properly subduing money, we will soon abuse and waste it all away. The prodigal son exhausted his father's inheritance because he had no appreciation for it. The Lord intends for us to develop gratitude towards our inheritance so we may be responsible with its value.

"And he entreated Abram well for her sake: and he had sheep, and oxen, and he asses, and menservants, and maidservants, and she asses, and camels…And Abram went up out of Egypt, he, and his wife, and all that he had, and Lot with him, into the south. And Abram was very rich in cattle, in silver, and in gold." (Genesis 12:16, 13:1, 2)

Notice here how Abraham came out rich! Abraham coming out of Egypt prosperous was the same manner the children of Israel exited as well. They came out spiritually sound and monetarily wealthy. The truth is, they had everything they would need *before* they entered the promised land.

This speaks profoundly of what transpired within our born-again spirit. We were made whole from the start! Just think about that for a moment. We are not waiting for what God promised to bring us completion: the promise of the Father is the Lamb who was slain! The baptism of the Holy Spirit and His residence within us would be His grand finale!

Inheriting the promised land is renewing our minds to the reality of what has already occurred within.

We will not be able to enjoy life with Jesus if we are still looking back to Egypt. So, the Lord is preparing us to inherit in the physical, that which has already occurred in the spirit.

There are great and mighty things the Lord has spoken to us all. There are desires He's placed within us that only He can fulfill. We must pursue Him to discover our future. However, let us not miss the purpose of our walk with God in the first place.

The goal is not to endlessly search for the gold at the end of the rainbow, only to realize we had it all from the start. He wants us to enjoy the journey of getting to know Him in route to the destination He's called us to. Jesus is the journey *and* the destination.

Let us fix our eyes on Jesus in the wilderness so we can experience all that He has for us now and all that He has for us to come. We will be thoroughly disappointed if we place all hope in our ministries, spouses, or dreams coming true… and miss Jesus throughout the journey.

To have a prosperous journey, we must leave our pasts behind. In Exodus, we find yet another similarity between us, and the children of Israel, when first leaving Egypt. We carry the burden of familiarity.

Unleavened Results

"And the people took their dough before it was leavened, their kneadingtroughs being bound up in their clothes upon their shoulders." *(Exodus 12:34)*

The *kneading troughs* the children of Israel carried with them were the instruments they used to make bread. Interestingly worded, the scripture says they were "bound up in their clothes on their shoulders."

The Lord spoke to me through this verse about familiarity.

See, we become familiar with the way things always seemed to have worked. We carry our "old ways" upon our shoulders. And when we find ourselves in a transition from where we've come, to where we're going, we may rely on the familiar way we "made bread."

As we continue reading, we see the Israelites couldn't attain the same results they were used to in Egypt:

"And they baked unleavened cakes of the dough which they brought forth out of Egypt, for it was not leavened; because they were thrust out of Egypt, and could not tarry, neither had they prepared for themselves any victual." *(Exodus 12:39)*

The children of Israel tried to make bread the way they were used to, but it wasn't working. They would soon realize they were going to have to lay down their works and gather the unmerited bread from heaven: manna. (We will be discussing this in greater detail in chapter 6: *What is this?*). Jesus was the substance of the manna given from heaven.

We must trust the bread the Lord is feeding us from now on. It may taste unfamiliar, but it's only for our benefit. This new bread would be without the pollution of sin. The leaven was left in the land for a reason; Jesus was looking to renew their minds with His word, and to purge them from the yeast of Egypt.

Leaven, or yeast, is used for this purpose: to rise. Now that we are "out of Egypt," we fix our eyes on the One who must rise on the throne of our hearts: the risen Christ. If we learn to be satisfied with Jesus alone, we will properly reign in the land flowing with milk and honey.

Looking Back

> *"Let thine eyes look right on, and let thine eyelids look straight before thee. Ponder the path of thy feet, and let all thy ways be established. Turn not to the right hand nor to the left: remove thy foot from evil." (Proverbs 4:25-27)*

Leaving Egypt is to refrain from looking back. The cares of life, and lusts of the flesh, have mostly to do with dwelling on where we came from.

> *"Now the LORD had said unto Abram, Get thee out of thy country, and from thy kindred, and from thy father's house, unto a land that I will shew thee." (Genesis 12:1)*

This is an admonition for us. Like the children of Israel came out of Egypt, and Abraham came out of Ur of the Chaldees, we came out of sin with the devil as our father. The book of Joshua speaks of the idolatrous nation Abraham came out of:

> *"And Joshua said unto all the people, Thus saith the LORD God of Israel, Your fathers dwelt on the other side of the flood in old time, even Terah, the father of Abraham, and the father of Nachor: **and they served other gods.**" (Joshua 24:2) (emphasis mine)*

We may have served sin on the other side of the flood, but we must consider our old man buried in the sea. Our false gods were destroyed, and the bondage of sin was broken. Nevertheless, if we neglect to behold Jesus, we can serve sin in our minds, and carry it out in our bodies.

> *"And truly, if they had been mindful of that country from whence they came out, they might have had opportunity to have returned." (Hebrews 11:15)*

Remember Lot? Remember his wife? Isn't it interesting how Abraham took Lot with him out of his country, and all that came from it was grief? Lot's righteous soul was vexed when he was dwelling in Sodom and Gomorrah.

In speculation, I believe this is an allegory for us. I believe Abraham taking Lot with him, and the grief it caused, is as us allowing our soul to dwell on the outskirts of the country of sin. Abraham should have left Lot in Ur of the Chaldees. Likewise, we can't be dwelling in Sodom in our minds, and the promised land at the same time. Our righteous soul will be vexed. We need to leave Lot behind!

"Now therefore fear the LORD, and serve him in sincerity and in truth: and put away the gods which your fathers served on the other side of the flood, and in Egypt; and serve ye the LORD." (Joshua 24:14)

Consider James' admonition:

"But every man is tempted, when he is drawn away of his own lust, and enticed. Then when lust hath conceived, it bringeth forth sin: and sin, when it is finished, bringeth forth death." (James 1:14, 15)

Being mindful of the country we came out of will lead us into temptation. When lust is entertained, the conception is sin. The only thing that's birthed from that union is death. Fleeting thoughts of sin will not cause you to fall (we are bombarded with contradictory things all the time), agreeing with, dwelling on, and *entertaining* the lust will cause sin and death. We must fix our eyes and train our ears to only acknowledge Jesus throughout all the noise.

"This I say then, Walk in the Spirit, and ye shall not fulfil the lust of the flesh. For the flesh lusteth against the Spirit, and the Spirit against the flesh: and these are contrary the one to the other: so that ye cannot do the things that ye would." (Galatians 5:16, 17)

We cannot focus on two things at once. We will either look back to Egypt and feed the flesh or look unto Jesus and walk in the Spirit. However, looking back in faith will propel us forward. That is, looking back to the cross of Jesus Christ. What we are to remember is His past, not ours. We consider the blood on the doorpost, not the food by the Nile River.

"For I determined not to know any thing among you, save Jesus Christ, and him crucified." (1ˢᵗ Corinthians 2:2)

If we look back, it's at the cross; when we look forward, it's on the resurrected Christ. If we look back, it's at the 12 stones taken out of the Jordan River… not Egypt. God wants us to focus on His deliverance, not what we left behind. Whether we look back, forward, up or down: the cross of Christ and the power of His resurrection is all that we should see.

Even if we wanted to go back to Egypt, we couldn't… so why go back there in our minds? Consider Stephen's testimony in the book of Acts:

"To whom our fathers would not obey, but thrust him from them, and in their hearts turned back again into Egypt." (Acts 7:39)

The children of Israel may have been camping in the wilderness, but in their hearts, still dwelling in Egypt. We know this is true because "out of the abundance of the heart the mouth speaks" (Matthew 12:34). And when the children of Israel spoke, they brought up their past lives in Egypt.

The Lord may have delivered the children of Israel out of Egypt, but He wanted to deliver the Egypt out of them.

"And it came to pass, when Pharaoh had let the people go, that God led them not through the way of the land of the Philistines, although that was near; for God said, Lest peradventure the people repent when they see war, and they return to Egypt: But God led the people about, through the way of the wilderness of the Red sea: and the children of Israel went up harnessed out of the land of Egypt." (Exodus 13:17, 18)

I like how the Lord said: "although that was near." As a good General, the Lord wasn't going to risk taking untrained warriors to battle. He was going to take them through a wilderness "Bootcamp." The focus of this training would be equipping them in belief as their manner of warfare. For this reason, it was of the utmost importance to have them repent from Egypt.

If the children of Israel had stood fast and believed God, they would have seen that He was fighting for them. When the Lord calls His people to battle, He slays most of the enemy Himself! From hailstones and fire, through fear and them turning on themselves, He is Jehovah Gibbor Milchama: *The Lord mighty in battle*! He was fighting for them; they were only called to believe.

God doesn't want us having one hand on the plow looking back. We'll lose our balance. Instability is the fruit of doublemindedness.

Now, if the enemy fails in having us look back, he'll want us to become stagnant. We must continue journeying forward! Nevertheless, going forward will cause our souls to count the cost. Our souls will try to subject us to what it wants and needs, but we must take authority over it. The goal is to have God's desires become our own. This will inevitably cause a weaning process:

"Surely I have behaved and quieted myself, as a child that is weaned of his mother: my soul is even as a weaned child." (Psalm 131:2)

Beholding the Lord will cause our souls to stir up dross:

"But who may abide the day of his coming? and who shall stand when he appeareth? for he is like a refiner's fire, and like fullers' soap: And he shall sit as a refiner and purifier of silver: and he shall purify the sons of Levi, and purge them as gold and silver, that they may offer unto the LORD an offering in righteousness." (Malachi 3:2, 3)

"Take away the dross from the silver, and there shall come forth a vessel for the finer." (Proverbs 25:4)

The Lord is refining, pruning, and preparing us for greatness. He is purging us from the ways of Egypt. We must only look to Him.

Walking With Christ Jesus

One thing to note is the better communion we have as New Testament believers. We look back to the Garden of Eden and think how much "better" it must have been. Truthfully, it was a paradise and must have been amazing! Even so, we have one thing they didn't: The Holy Spirit now lives within us! He walks with us in the garden of our hearts. Jesus, the Last Adam and true Gardener, now does the work within.

We also think of how much better it must have been to have walked with Jesus as the disciples did. Without a doubt, it must have been awesome! Any one of us would have wanted to do that same thing. Yet He said it was *better* that He departed so the Comforter could come (John 16:7).

Keep in mind, Paul (the one who hadn't walked with Jesus) was often teaching the disciples who had walked with him. That's why Paul would often address the Lord as Christ Jesus, whereas the apostles referred to Him as Jesus Christ. The apostles knew Jesus as the Man first, and then the Christ. Paul knew Him as Christ first, then walked with Him in the Spirit.

"Whom having not seen, ye love; in whom, though now ye see him not, yet believing, ye rejoice with joy unspeakable and full of glory." (1 Peter 1:8)

We haven't seen Jesus in the flesh, nor did we see Him die on the cross… yet we walk with Him, nonetheless. Walking with Jesus is available for all today!

While Jesus was on the earth in His physical body, He was subject to being in only one place at one time. People would travel many miles to find Him. Now, we have access to Him 24/7. We can charge right into the throne room!

Every foreshadow of the Old Testament was satisfied with the substance we can now enjoy forever. Mainly walking with Jesus.

Consider the benefits of the initial Passover. For one, the children of Israel spent 40 years in the desert with clothing and sandals that never ruined. There also wasn't one sick or weak among them! Furthermore, the blood on the doorpost granted them protection, favor, wholeness, and supernatural provision. If the portrait of Christ enabled them to live whole the *moment* they stepped foot out of Egypt, how much more now for us?

The children of Israel came out as one after eating the Passover. Now more than ever, the body of Christ needs to step out as one. For this cause, Paul wrote about unity in his letter to the Corinthian church. He addressed their irreverent drunkenness at the communion table and rebuked them for their ignorance of the body and blood of Jesus.

Discerning The Body

"…Take, eat: this is my body, which is broken for you…" (1st Corinthians 11:24)

There were two significant errors concerning the manner the Corinthians ate and drank. First, they weren't preferring and discerning each other as being the Lord's body. Secondly, they weren't discerning Jesus' literal body broken for us.

*"For he that eateth and drinketh unworthily, eateth and drinketh damnation to himself, **not discerning the Lord's body. For this cause many are weak and sickly among you, and many sleep**." (1st Corinthians 11:29, 30) (emphasis mine)*

"And when he had given thanks, he brake it, and said, Take, eat: this is my body, which is broken for you: this do in remembrance of me. After the same manner also he took the cup, when he had supped, saying, this cup is the new testament in my blood: this do ye, as oft as ye drink it, in remembrance of me." (1st Corinthians 11:24, 25)

There were many weak and sick among them. Why? Because they weren't discerning the Lord's body. They weren't eating and drinking in remembrance of Him. Therefore, when we discern the Lord's body, we need to *remember* what happened.

Jesus took the full punishment for our sin, and His righteous soul became an offering (Isaiah 53:10). His back was ripped apart for us (Isaiah 53:4-5, 1st Peter 2:24, Isaiah 50:6). He was violently beaten with cat-o-nine tails, which exposed all His bones (Psalm 22:17). While dying on the cross, the soldiers who had a hand in placing Him there carelessly gambled for His garments (Psalm 22:18). His beard was plucked out and His face was spit upon (Isaiah 50:6). A thorny crown was then pressed into His skull.

After His cruel and merciless beating, they placed a purple robe on His raw and tender body (John 19:2). He was scourged and marred beyond recognition (Isaiah 52:14). He was mocked, scorned, humiliated, rejected, and despised. He hung naked on a cross where they pierced His hands and feet (Psalm 22:16). His bones were out of joint; His heart was like melted wax, and the wicked compassed Him about while shaking their heads (Psalm 22:7, 14, 16).

All this to say, we deserved death, and He didn't. He died on *our* cross. He took upon Himself all sin, sickness and disease (Isaiah 53:4, 10, Psalm 107:20).

The Father also turned away His head for a moment (Isaiah 54:7), causing Him to cry:

"...Eli, Eli, lama sabachthani? that is to say, My God, My God, why hast thou forsaken me?" Matthew 27:46

This was quoted from the beginning of Psalm 22: the crucifixion psalm. The Jews would've been able to recite this whole psalm in their heart. They could have seen the Christ before their eyes fulfill the whole thing... if they cared to. Through all this, He cried:

"...Father, forgive them; for they know not what they do..." (Luke 23:34)

For us, His joy, He endured the cross. Selah.

Thank you, Jesus. *This* is our communion of Him. We are to remember Him and the price that He paid. He is the broken bread and the wine poured out for us. If we partake in this manner, we are eating and drinking worthily, and will properly discern the Lord's body.

How can we take communion of Him and be in unforgiveness towards our brother? Jesus died so that we may be one with Him, and that we may be one with each other. We are all the bride of Christ, and His many-membered body.

Chapter Four

Bitter Waters

"And whosoever shall give to drink unto one of these little ones a cup of cold water only in the name of a disciple, verily I say unto you, he shall in no wise lose his reward." (Matthew 10:42)

In this chapter, we will discuss the pure water of God's word.

"Wherewithal shall a young man cleanse his way? by taking heed thereto according to thy word." (Psalm 119:9)

The word of God is likened to many things. For one, it is compared to a seed. Here we are today because we believed in the seed of truth!

His word is light. The light of His word expels darkness, brings to life the seeds that are sown and provides us with direction.

Amongst many other comparisons: His word is like a hammer; His word is like a fire; His word is like a sword; His word is like honey, and His word is like water. The word of God is simply the most wonderful gift God has given unto man, second of course, to our salvation.

Psalm 119 is beautifully and purposefully written, arranged in an acrostic pattern, with the relentless focus on heeding God's word. Through mention of God's precepts, laws, statutes and commands, His testimonies, His judgments, His ways and His word: we are left with the realization that God's word, truly, is the only way a man can cleanse his way.

The Plagues Of Moses And The Miracles Of Jesus

The account of Jesus turning water into wine is an astounding parallel to the first plague performed by Moses in Egypt. Also, the Israelite's arriving at Marah on the third day goes hand in hand.

As I was sitting at the dinner table with a friend one day, he brought up a point that stuck with me for good. He said:

"David, do you know what the first plague Moses executed upon the Egyptians was?"

I answered, *"yes, turning the water into blood?"*

He replied, *"yes; and Jesus' first miracle was turning water into wine."*

Wow, what an insight! Remarkably, upon the instant I heard this, I was shown by the Holy Spirit the latter part of this revelation, and responded:

"Raphael, the last plague performed by Moses upon the Egyptians was the death of their firstborn sons, and the last act of Jesus on this earth was His death... which was the death of the firstborn Son!"

We were overjoyed for the Lord to have revealed such an awesome connection.

Upon further discussion, Raphael and I gleaned how these two accounts not only correlated but also contrasted. Though the first and last plague of Moses, paralleled the first and last miracle of Jesus, the difference was clear: Moses executed judgment upon Egypt, but Jesus took the judgment upon Himself.

To further appreciate what Jesus did for us, here are a few scriptures to bring to light concerning judgment:

"For the Father judgeth no man, but hath committed all judgment unto the Son." John 5:22

When first reading this passage, it may appear that Jesus judges us on the Father's behalf. The proper interpretation of this passage, however, is how the Father *placed* all judgment upon the Son. The judgment the Father committed to the Son, was the judgment of sin in His body (1st Peter 2:24, 2nd Corinthians 5:21).

"And as Moses lifted up the serpent in the wilderness, even so must the Son of man be lifted up: That whosoever believeth in him should not perish, but have eternal life." (John 3:14, 15)

*"Now is the judgment of this world: now shall the prince of this world be cast out. And I, if I be lifted up from the earth, will draw all **men** unto me." (John 12:31, 32)*

In the King James Bible, *men* is italicized in John 12:32, because it's not found in Greek. The translators added words when necessary for readability. This is common because of various word meanings and idioms not found in the translated language. To show when these words were added, they were placed in italics. Without the word men, it reads: *will draw all unto me*. This passage is better interpreted by *judgment* being what's drawn unto Him, because of the passage right before it.

Jesus was about to go to the cross. He would then take the judgment of the world upon Himself. In a sense, Jesus became a lightning rod for God's wrath to strike.

As the burnt sacrifice was utterly consumed upon the altar, so was Jesus. I believe this is also one reason He may have said, *"I thirst"* (John 19:28). Along with being severely dehydrated from the loss of blood and bodily fluids, He was also experiencing the fiery judgment of God in our stead!

Additionally, moments before Jesus cried it was finished, He received a sponge full of vinegar. This sponge was placed upon a hyssop stalk and then put to His mouth. This account led me to consider the Israelites' arrival at Marah:

"And when they came to Marah, they could not drink of the waters of Marah, for they were bitter: therefore the name of it was called Marah. And the people murmured against Moses, saying, What shall we drink?" (Exodus 15:23, 24)

Like a sponge, Jesus soaked up the bitter waters for us.

Interestingly with hyssop, it was used in ceremonial cleansing rituals as required under the law of Moses. It was also dipped in a basin of blood and struck upon the doorposts on the night of the Passover. Jesus, the Door, was struck for us!

All ceremony and sacrifice, of course, only foreshadowed the One to come. The blood of bulls and goats were insufficient. Truly, our fallen nature could never be cleansed through the blood of an animal; only the water and blood from Jesus' side could make us pure:

"But one of the soldiers with a spear pierced his side, and forthwith came there out blood and water. And he that saw it bare record, and his record is true: and he knoweth that he saith true, that ye might believe." (John 19:34, 35)

Jesus was the substance of all ceremonies performed in the Old Testament. He would taste the bitterness of death for us, and swallow it in victory. He took God's wrath on the cross as the Lamb of God slain in our place. Hallelujah!

To conclude with what we originally discussed concerning the plagues and the miracles, Moses' staff will shed some light on the cross of Christ.

"Thus saith the LORD, In this thou shalt know that I am the LORD: behold, I will smite with the rod that is in mine hand upon the waters which are in the river, and they shall be turned to blood." (Exodus 7:17)

Moses' staff stretched upon the waters that turned into blood, was the foreshadowing of the cross of Christ, and His blood being poured out for us.

Like the river that turned into blood affected all the water sources in Egypt, so did the water and blood that poured out of Jesus' side affect all of us. Our true water source was cut off at the fall, but because of the river of blood and water flowing from Calvary's hill, our wells have been redeemed! We applied the blood of Jesus to our broken cisterns and received from a whole new source.

Waters Made Sweet

They have no wine...

"And it shall come to pass, if they will not believe also these two signs, neither hearken unto thy voice, that thou shalt take of the water of the river, and pour it upon the dry land: and the water which thou takest out of the river shall become blood upon the dry land." (Exodus 4:9)

The third sign would be the dry land receiving the water turned into blood. The number three is significant in the Bible, and almost always refers to Jesus' death, burial, and resurrection.

*"So Moses brought Israel from the Red sea, and they went out into the wilderness of Shur: and they went three days in the wilderness, and found no water...And he cried unto the LORD; and the LORD shewed him a tree, which when he had cast into the waters, **the waters were made sweet**: there he made for them a statute and an ordinance, and there he proved them." (Exodus 15:22, 25) (emphasis mine)*

What stands out in this passage is how on the third day, the waters were made "sweet". Keep this in mind as I refer to Jesus' invitation to the wedding in Cana.

*"And the **third day** there was a marriage in Cana of Galilee; and the mother of Jesus was there: and both Jesus was called, and his disciples, to the marriage. And when they wanted wine, the mother of Jesus saith unto him, They have no wine. Jesus saith unto her, Woman, what have I to do with thee? mine hour is not yet come." (John 2:1-4) (emphasis mine)*

What a mysterious response from Jesus in this instance, yet in scripture, it is not uncommon to find Him responding either with another question, or a redirected statement. It seems He answers the questions they *should* have asked. Sometimes we read and wonder:

"Lord, why did you respond that way? Your answer is another parable of some sort!"

The scripture in Proverbs comes to mind:

"It is the glory of God to conceal a thing: but the honour of kings is to search out a matter." (Proverbs 25:2)

With Jesus' response, it seems He answered His mother in a hidden message by saying: *"My hour isn't here yet."*

Consider what that hour may have been. Was it the beginning of His ministry perhaps? Did Mary provoke Him into starting His ministry prematurely? Was He prophesying the hour of His death? Could the hour Jesus referred to, be the hour His kingdom would be settled on the earth? Well, if we continue in the book of John, we find the answer:

*"And Jesus answered them, saying, The **hour** is come, that the Son of man should be glorified. Verily, verily, I say unto you, Except a corn of wheat fall into the ground and **die**, it abideth alone: **but if it die**, it bringeth forth much fruit." (John 12:23, 24) (emphasis mine)*

Clearly, the hour Jesus referred to was His death. He responded to Mary concerning His death before His ministry even began! Why? This is where journeying to Marah ties into Jesus performing His first miracle. He was really saying: *"I will soon make the bitter waters sweet for mankind to drink from, by offering my life on the tree."*

69

Moses was told to cast the tree into the bitter waters, which caused them to turn sweet. The best wine was the sweetest of all in the end! Before His ministry even began, He was foretelling us of His blood being poured out at Calvary.

"...Every man at the beginning doth set forth good wine; and when men have well drunk, then that which is worse: but thou hast kept the good wine until now." (John 2:10)

When Mary said, *"they have no wine,"* Jesus responded according to what would be His final act, through His first miracle: His blood and water being poured out of His side for everyone to drink. For the joy set before Him, He endured the cross! As the people rejoiced for His wine at the wedding, so is there a celebration in heaven for every sinner that repents.

Water Pots Of Stone

"And there was set there six waterpots of stone, after the manner of the purifying of the Jews, containing two or three firkins apiece." (John 2:6)

The water pots Jesus used to transform the water into wine were extremely significant. First, we learn from scripture how the number six represents man:

"Here is wisdom. Let him that hath understanding count the number of the beast: for it is the number of a man, and his number is Six hundred threescore and six." (Revelation 13:18)

We also know from scripture that man was created on the sixth day:

"So God created man in his own image, in the image of God created he him; male and female created he them...And the evening and the morning were the sixth day." (Genesis 1:27, 31)

When God created man, He intended their source to have been Him.

"Jesus saith unto them, Fill the waterpots with water. And they filled them up to the brim." (John 2:7)

By ourselves, we can never "do" enough, be "filled" enough, or "clean" enough. Without Jesus, we can never have our lives filled to the brim, according to His word. We'll always be left with a few measures of the world's waters in substitution. Only He can transform our stony water pots into vessels of new wine. The waters of this world can never satisfy; His blood is the only source of purification.

"And no man putteth new wine into old bottles: else the new wine doth burst the bottles, and the wine is spilled, and the bottles will be marred: but new wine must be put into new bottles." (Mark 2:22)

It's also important to note the process of new wine being poured into new bottles. In fact, it's not a bottle at all. It is the skin of an animal that holds the wine… a *wineskin*. Consider how it's not the wine conforming to the shape of the bottle, but it is the wineskin conforming to the wine. In other words, we must conform to God's word and have it shape us the way He sees fit, not the other way around.

Old wineskins were those that were no longer used. As a result, they would become dry and brittle. Interestingly, the way they would create "new" skins, would be to submerge them in water, and rub olive oil upon them until flexible again. What an amazing parallel for us! We must submerge ourselves in the water of God's word, and allow the oil and power of the Holy Ghost to transform us.

Born Of Flesh Is Flesh, Born Of Spirit Is Spirit

How can a man be born when he is old?

Becoming born-again is something Jesus told Nicodemus was necessary to see the kingdom of God:

"Jesus answered and said unto him, Verily, verily, I say unto thee, Except a man be born again, he cannot see the kingdom of God. Nicodemus saith unto him, How can a man be born when he is old? Can he enter the second time into his mother's womb, and be born? Jesus answered, Verily, verily, I say unto thee, Except a man be born of water and of the Spirit, he cannot enter into the kingdom of God. That which is born of the flesh is flesh; and that which is born of the Spirit is spirit. Marvel not that I said unto thee, Ye must be born again." (John 3:3-7)

This was brought to light for what we'll discuss next: Jesus washing His disciples' feet.

An error in the church culture today is that we need to "recommit" our lives unto Jesus. This doctrine is crippling because it causes us to follow Jesus with a sin-conscience. God wants us to live with a conscience that is, "without offense towards God and man" (Acts 24:16).

> *"And Paul, earnestly beholding the council, said, Men and brethren, I have lived in all good conscience before God until this day. And the high priest Ananias commanded them that stood by him to smite him on the mouth." (Acts 23:1, 2)*

The religious will slap you for saying something like that! How dare we even think of such a thing! Nevertheless, this is how God truly desires us to live. The enemy would love for you to walk around with a guilty conscience, but not the Lord. Consider one of my favorite explanations of a sin-conscience through scripture:

> *"For the law having a shadow of good things to come, and not the very image of the things, can never with those sacrifices which they offered year by year continually make the comers thereunto perfect. For then would they not have ceased to be offered? Because the worshippers once purged should have had no more conscience of sins. But in those sacrifices there is a remembrance again made of sins every year." (Hebrews 10:1-3)*

This is an important concept to understand. If the need for sacrifice caused the remembrance of sin year by year, where was the freedom? The freedom would be in the true Sacrifice to come! Not in an animal's blood (which left you in need of another sacrifice, and caused you to remember *sin* again): but in the blood of Jesus alone. Once for all; past, present, and future.

Concerning the urge to recommit our lives to Christ, it was adopted into our culture through fear. Fear of not being right with God, and fear of dying in sin. *"So, we must confess our sins daily and recommit our lives to Jesus as often as necessary... only to be sure we're truly saved..."* This is simply not the case. This mindset causes us to miss out on our salvation altogether by thinking we may lose it.

Even if we don't believe we will lose our salvation, we certainly lose the joy of it. It's more like living in a state of eternal condemnation than a state of eternal life. It's simply one of the most crippling doctrines in the body of Christ today. It is fear-based, not faith-based. And we know whatever is not done in faith is sin to begin with (Romans 14:23).

Most of us will agree that it's not as if you can simply fall into sin and blaspheme the Holy Spirit, (Now, I do believe you can forfeit your salvation, but it is not my intention to discuss that in this book; my intention is to discuss the joy of living without condemnation), yet some of us believe that we should have an "altar" call every now and then, just to ensure we're right with God. This behavior will cause you to lose your confidence and approach God in unbelief.

Just as a baby cannot be "re-born" in their mother's womb, we cannot be "re-born" again in the Spirit. Either we are born-again into the kingdom of God once, or we never have been in the first place. You are not "re-saved" every time you recommit your life at the altar.

Most born-again believers will condemn themselves greater than anyone else on the planet. We do more harm to ourselves than the devil does altogether. We do most of the work for him!

Before Christ, the Jewish people lived with a clearer conscience than most believers do today. They were only reminded of their sins at the altar. Even then, the sacrifice itself was inspected for spot or blemish, not the one offering it… foreshadowing the freedom that would be found in beholding the sinless Lamb! Jesus was inspected for us and was found without fault.

Then said Pilate to the chief priests and to the people, I find no fault in this man." (Luke 23:4)

What the author of Hebrews implied was if the Jews had such a Lamb, they should have no longer remembered their sins, but should have been perfected.

We have been perfected in the spirit, and the power is in the resurrection.

Living with a sin-conscience is like stepping foot into a broken shackle with a dragging chain. It's time to lay aside the weight and walk in the liberty of Christ. We need to recognize our old man as crucified with Him. Stop recommitting your life at the altar; *refocus* on the resurrected Christ, and let the joy of the Lord be your continual strength.

Will You Wash My feet, Lord?

As the prophets of old sensed their time coming to an end, they would declare and administer the things of the utmost importance.

Jacob prophesied and blessed his sons; Moses commanded Joshua of the battles ahead; David anointed Solomon and declared the way to build the temple; Jesus ate with his disciples and washed their feet.

In the gospel of John, the Lord washed each of His disciples' feet, yet found resistance when approaching Peter's. The following will be the summary of this account found in the thirteenth chapter.

Peter, astounded as Jesus knelt at his feet, uttered: *"Lord... are you intending to wash my feet?"*

Jesus explained: *"You won't understand what I'm doing at the moment, but will afterward."*

Peter unknowingly said something he, nor we should ever consider: *"Lord, You will never wash my feet."*

Jesus then said plainly: *"If I don't wash you, you'll have no part with Me."*

After a brief counsel within himself, Peter proposed something we may have all said in that moment: *"Lord, not only my feet... but my hands and my head too!"*

I could imagine Peter speculating: *"If all the disciples are having their feet washed... I'm sure if my whole body is washed, I'll have the greatest part!"*

Lovingly, and full of wisdom, Jesus responded: *"He that is washed doesn't need to be cleansed again... except for his feet."*

After the cleansing was completed, Jesus sat down again, concluding: *"...Do you know what I have just done? You call me Master and Lord, and you say this truthfully, because I am. If I then, your Lord and Master, have washed your feet, you should also wash one another's feet. For I have given you an example that you should do unto others, as I have done unto you."*

There is much here that can be expounded upon, but let's focus on one thing Jesus said for now: *"He that is washed is clean overall, but still needs to wash his feet."*

Notice how Jesus didn't oblige Peter's request, or commend him for his zeal; He said he only needed to have his feet washed. This is because as we walk in this world, we attract dust. Jesus is the word made flesh, and the word began to wash His disciples' feet.

"That he might sanctify and cleanse it with the washing of water by the word." (Ephesians 5:26)

John 15:3 says: *"Now ye are clean through the word which I have spoken to you."*

Jesus is speaking about the washing of our feet in likeness to our minds being washed by His word. We must be cleansed daily due to the spiritual bombardment we're exposed to in our everyday walk. This is vital that we do what Jesus commanded:

"For I have given you an example, that ye should do as I have done to you." (John 13:15)

Which is: allowing Jesus to wash our minds with the water of His word.

Jesus was portraying the fact that you don't need to become born again, *again*, but rather, allow the word to wash away the daily dust of unbelief that accumulates by default in this fallen world.

Remember what happened in the Garden of Eden? The serpent was cursed and would have to slither on its belly eating dust all the days of its life. Allowing Jesus to wash us with His word will starve the serpent, because dust is what he feeds on!

We often can't see the dirt that accumulates on our body, but we know it's necessary to take a shower. Likewise, we may not see the accumulation of unbelief, but it's surely a substance only dealt with by His word. As faith comes by hearing God's word, unbelief comes by hearing everything that contradicts it.

Additionally, when the apostles went out in two's and weren't received, they could *"shake the dust off their feet"* by speaking the truth over each other.

Our feet are the only body parts that continuously touch the earth, so this was the perfect example Jesus could have given. Walk around with sandals and your feet will get dusty!

Jesus took care of our sin nature and washed us in His blood once for all. That's why it isn't necessary to receive any other sacrifice or have Him die each time we sin. We simply need our feet washed daily.

One last thought. When we take a shower, we don't try to identify with the dust or where it came from. We don't think: *"Well, this dirt came from work. This dust came from here. This dust came from there. Oh, this dust... sure, that's some dusty dust."*

As funny as this may sound, consider the point: when taking a shower, we just apply the water, and the dust is taken care of. We just need to jump in! Now, if we go without a shower for a few days, we can see the repercussions. Therefore, we must follow this example and shower every day. In doing so, we will keep the ground of our hearts pure.

Overtaken

Jesus told His disciples to beware of the doctrines of the religious leaders of the day, as to not allow what was being taught by Him to become polluted. He didn't want them overtaken by anything rising in place of God's word alone.

> *"And he charged them, saying, Take heed, beware of the leaven of the Pharisees, and of the leaven of Herod. And they reasoned among themselves, saying, It is because we have no bread." (Mark 8:15, 16)*

Isn't it interesting how even at that moment they couldn't perceive what He was saying? The enemy was at work even then! God's words, and the potential they have in the hearts of believers, have been under attack since the garden of Eden: *"Hath God said?"*

If the enemy can get you to believe something other than what God has said, you'll reap a harvest of unbelief.

The Bible says that the word of God is pure. For this reason, the enemy is after the word being sown in our hearts. He is trying to stop the union of the seed and our hearts altogether. We are not persecuted for *our* sake, we are persecuted for the w*ord's* sake.

We know that the word of God is an incorruptible seed. So, the enemy can only try to stop the 30, 60 and 100-fold increase… if we allow him. Not allowing Jesus to wash our feet will permit the enemy to spoil our harvest.

Interesting to note, the enemy cannot steal the seed before it has the chance to be understood. The fowls aren't flying around catching seeds in their mouths. The word must have the potential to be believed before it can be stolen.

> *"Hear ye therefore the parable of the sower. When any one heareth the word of the kingdom, and understandeth it not, then cometh the wicked one, and catcheth away that which was sown in his heart. This is he which received seed by the way side." (Matthew 13:18, 19)*

Being that the enemy cannot pollute the seed, he will come after the ground if unsuccessful in his attempt to steal it.

The parable of the sower is really all about the ground!

The enemy wants to pollute the ground of our hearts with deceit. He wants to consume us with care. The father of lies has been at work since the first garden, where the first man fell. He wants us to fall after the same manner of doubt and unbelief.

Consider Shammah. He was one of David's mighty men who stood his ground over a lentil patch. This account is found in the book of second Samuel.

Shammah knew that if he didn't guard the small patch, the enemy would overtake the whole garden. The enemy is after the small seed that's sown because God is after the abundant harvest.

"But when the fruit is brought forth, immediately he putteth in the sickle, because the harvest is come." (Mark 4:29)

The Lord is after the fruit immediately! The fruit is not always immediate, but when ripe… the sickle is! That's why we'll surely reap if we just hold on. We must endure until the harvest.

"And let us not be weary in well doing: for in due season we shall reap, if we faint not." (Galatians 6:9)

You only need to let the tree you've planted come to maturity to receive fruit; you don't have to keep planting one every time you want an apple. That's why it is so important to never lose hope. In hope and patience, we see the promise through.

"Hope deferred maketh the heart sick: but when the desire cometh, it is a tree of life." (Proverbs 13:12)

Now, if the enemy fails to halt conception, he'll settle for the stony ground. This is the second ground. This one gladly receives the word, yet has no root within. It succumbs to offense and quickly withers away. (We will discuss offense in greater detail in chapter six: *What is this?*).

The third ground is that of care and concern. The enemy will try to overtake you with the leaven of worry, the deceitfulness of riches, and the pride of life. All to rob the attention of what really matters. All to take the place of the Lord's.

If the enemy is successful in his third attempt, the lentil patch will be overtaken, and you'll lose your harvest. That's why:

"No man that warreth entangleth himself with the affairs of this life..."
(2nd Timothy 2:4)

If the mighty man of David were to lose his focus, the lentil patch would have been overtaken. What a seemingly small thing to guard with your life! Well, this man represents us, because we are one of Jesus' mighty men! Therefore, we must guard our heart with *all* diligence (Proverbs 4:23).

Care is what the enemy bombards us with. For this reason, Jesus says to be anxious for nothing. The ground overtaken with care, is the one right before the 30, 60 and 100-fold harvest!

In speculation, I believe most Christians fall short at the third ground. They are right about to reap a harvest, but at the last moment they succumb to fear. Their hope is aborted, and faith no longer has any substance to bring forth. They were so close, yet overtaken. We mustn't let care consume us!

"Let not your heart be troubled: ye believe in God, believe also in me."
(John 14:1)

We mustn't *let* our hearts be troubled. We must cast our care upon Him because He cares for us. If we choose to believe God's word alone and to disregard all the cunningly devised plans of the enemy, we will always reap the promise.

Well, the gospel wouldn't be the good news, unless there was some *really* good news! Matthew 13:33 says: *"The Kingdom of Heaven is like unto leaven, which a woman took, and hid it in three measures of meal, till the whole was leavened."*

Hallelujah! We have a more powerful leaven!

We can either let the leaven of the world overtake us, or the leaven of the word. One way or the other, we will be overtaken.

Lastly, what makes the ground good? What causes the *good* ground to produce? It's the absence of hard ground, the absence of stones, and the lack of care. The good ground is a heart that only believes God's word. It is a carefree ground. It is a heart full of hope and expectation in God alone.

When it comes to our ground, we need to be care-takers, not takers of care. If we take care of our ground, the fruit will come, but if we take care *into* our grounds, we will faint before the harvest.

Magnified

"Neither have I gone back from the commandment of his lips; I have esteemed the words of his mouth more than my necessary food." (Job 23:12)

When we place the highest value on the word of God, it becomes our highest priority.

By words the worlds were formed. By a word, the sea is held back from going any farther. Through a word being preached, you believed. By a word out of your mouth, you confessed Jesus as Lord. Through words, you can change someone's entire life; and through negative words believed, someone can take their own. Death and life are in the power of the tongue.

The spoken word of God is the most powerful force on the planet. In fact, before the Holy Ghost overshadowed Mary, and she conceived, she said: "...Behold the handmaid of the Lord; be it unto me according to thy word." (Luke 1:38)

Mary conceived the word of God by confessing the word.

Through all the spoken words of prophets, kings, shepherds and commoners: Jesus, the word, was birthed on the earth.

Regarding the word, there is one scripture that I find fascinating. It seems to stand alone amongst the rest. It is found within a Psalm of David:

"I will worship toward thy holy temple, and praise thy name for thy lovingkindness and thy truth: for thou hast magnified thy word above all thy name." (Psalm 138:2)

Everything on earth has a name: *Table*, *chair*, the *ground*, the *sky*. The visible, and the invisible things, the things on the earth, and the things that are in heaven; inanimate objects and things with breath: they all have a name. We all have names: *Kathy, Melissa, John, Shane, Tony*. Even the word *name* is a word. Within this world framed with words, there is one thing higher than every other word, and every other name: the name of *Jesus*.

Hallelujah, to the name of Jesus!

"Wherefore God also hath highly exalted him, and given him a name which is above every name: That at the name of Jesus every knee should bow, of things in heaven, and things in the earth, and things under the earth; and that every tongue should confess that Jesus Christ is Lord, to the glory of God the Father." (Philippians 2:9-11)

In consideration of the things that are named on the earth, and the name of Jesus far exceeding all else, there is yet one thing higher than that: *His word.*

"...for thou hast magnified thy word above all thy name." (Psalm 138:2)

God magnified His word above His own name.

"My covenant will I not break, nor alter the thing that is gone out of my lips." (Psalm 89:34)

This is the standard He has placed upon Himself. We ought to place a higher standard on His word than our own names as well.

Well Counsel

"The word must impact us, before we can impact others."

When ministering, I am always touching on the importance of God's word. Any chance I get, I am pointing whoever I am speaking with back to the Bible. It's all about Jesus, and that's where He is found.

Effective ministry is drawing the gifting out from whom you're counseling, not having them rely on yours.

Most professional counselors will offer you advice as they see fit. Scheduling a session in the first place would imply that you cannot see what's fit, hence the need for advice the way someone else does.

Upon appointment, you'll be welcomed into their office and asked to share what's going on in your life. Their intentions are good, and they're well qualified to suggest the best course of action for you. However, this type of counsel is logical and not necessarily Biblical.

This counselor will offer you advice from their perspective in the hopes of persuading your own will and conscience. This will leave you with a glass of water from their own soul, rather than from the well within your own spirit. You will then require another glass from their source the next time you're thirsty.

Now, to be clear: truth is truth. You don't have to be a clinical psychologist to speak truth to someone. We are to be lovers of the truth, and always desirous to share and receive it.

With that said, when is any particular truth applicable? If you went to your ten friends for advice, and received ten different opinions… which truth should you adhere to? Was it Andrew's glass of water? Was it Anna's? Was it the glass of water Timothy provided?

Let's consider the counsel spoken of in the Bible:

"Counsel in the heart of man is like deep water; but a man of understanding will draw it out." (Proverbs 20:5)

The Proverbs counsel is that of a wise man drawing out from *you* the answer that's already within.

I used to read this scripture in this context: I had to have the understanding to draw the wisdom out of the well of the counselor's heart. The truth is, I already have the counsel within my heart, and a man of understanding will draw it out of me!

True Biblical counsel should always confirm and bare witness within the well of your own spirit. After consulting with an advisor, you shouldn't be left with only reason or logic guiding your decision; you should have been guided to the tap of the Holy Ghost's wisdom within your own cistern. This way you're not merely persuaded by someone else's advice, but confidently convinced of God's will for yourself.

This is not to say that we cannot receive someone's advice or opinion, or that professional counselors are inadequate. This is also not to say that it's wrong to draw the wisdom out from another. I do believe this scripture can apply both ways. However, principally, I believe that it is better interpreted by skillfully guiding someone to the answer that's *already* within. We're just guiding them to the light switch in their own bedroom.

We should covet prophesy and always desire prophetic ministry. This way, we are relying on God's wisdom and discernment for the brother or sister in whom we're ministering to. We have all the wisdom we will ever need within the well of our own spirit. Therefore, we should speak in a prophetic manner to stir up the well within them. If this is the manner you give or receive counsel, you'll be considered "a man of understanding."

David Ravella

Chapter Five

Wilderness

Part One

"Shew me thy ways, O LORD; teach me thy paths. Lead me in thy truth, and teach me: for thou art the God of my salvation; on thee do I wait all the day." (Psalms 25:4, 5)

The wilderness is where we must keep the promise our focus, and our past a fleeting thought. We've come out of Egypt and we're now in transition. Our soul is caught in the middle and must be renewed according to who we are and where we're going. Everyone has a wilderness period; it is purposed by God. The wilderness is not a place of wandering but is better defined as a preparation process.

This is where the Lord transforms our minds, purges unbelief, stirs and builds faith, and causes patience to have her perfect work… if we will allow Him.

It is not a 40-year period of murmuring and complaining, but a time set apart to lay the foundation of godly character. It is the caterpillar in the cocoon. It is a time of metamorphosis. It is a time of… time.

Anyone who has ever done anything significant for the Lord has undergone great preparation. God uses this period to equip us for what's ahead.

This chapter will be dedicated to the process in which the Lord chastises His children and instills within us the ability, and responsibility, to reign over our inheritance. We will discuss the giants on the other side waiting, and *how* they are waiting. We will talk about the law and its' purpose and how it ushered in Joshua. We will discuss Moses and how he greatly relates to Christ. We will address the proper way to resist temptation, and we will discuss the benefits of waiting on the Lord.

Time

> *"But they that wait upon the LORD shall renew their strength; they shall mount up with wings as eagles; they shall run, and not be weary; and they shall walk, and not faint." (Isaiah 40:31)*

How are we waiting on God? Are we submitting to the process? Are we squandering our time and resources on fruitless endeavors? *Hoary* is an old English term used to describe an elder with a gray head of hair:

> *"The hoary head is a crown of glory, if it be found in the way of righteousness." (Proverbs 16:31)*

Time will have only benefited the elder, had they chosen to spend it with God. Time, in and of itself, will not produce the promise, faith *and* patience will.

> *"Keep thy heart with all diligence; for out of it are the issues of life." (Proverbs 4:23)*

As we wait on the Lord, keeping our heart is the most important thing! If we were to prioritize a list of scriptures from one to ten, this wouldn't be number nine: it would be number one. Keeping watch over what enters our hearts should be the top priority of a believer.

(This is vital because the heart is *always* believing. For with the heart man believes... (Romans 10:10). It just depends on what you're believing! Like the earth is ready to receive seed, whether weeds or fruitful plants, so is the ground of our heart. Whatever enters in will be brought to life.)

There is only so much space we can occupy in our minds. As we think in our hearts, so are we (Proverbs 23:7). Therefore, we must guard what comes into our hearts with everything we've got. We will wind up becoming what we think upon the most. That's the point: we must think about Christ the most!

> *"Let this mind be in you, which was also in Christ Jesus." (Philippians 2:5)*

We are learning to be like Him by beholding Him. In return, we are experiencing the fruit of the Holy Ghost: patience. Patience is one of the most essential attributes of a leader. If we are to be His ambassadors and represent Him to the world, then without exception, we must be patient. Why? Because God is Love, and love, first of all, is patient.

God doesn't *have* love, He *is* Love; and as He is, so are we. God is love, and so are we! Therefore, we must understand patience because it's who God is! The Lord doesn't want the people He's gifted to be as shooting stars that burn up either through pride or pressure; He wants to establish North Stars in the sky that remain steadfast and bright. He is working in us the fruit of patience, and it cannot be hurried.

He is ever working on the foundation of our character to support our gifting adequately. Though the foundation is unseen, it's the most essential. What good is the biggest house on the block if it's starting to collapse in on itself? I have often prayed:

"Lord, I submit to You and the process. I ask You to do the foundational work necessary to sustain whatever You would like to build on top of it. Take the time now and equip me for the long-term."

Did you know the roots of a tree are just as tall under the ground as the canopy above? You only see half the tree above the ground. The other half is just as big and just as important... if not more important. The depth of the preparation is equivalent to the height of the calling.

Now, during this time set apart, we're not merely "waiting" on God (as if to say we're just sitting on the couch with our hands in our pockets), we're waiting on Him through service. Before the children of Israel entered the promised land, they had many journeys in the wilderness. Though we may not have it all mapped out, we're always going *somewhere* with God. Wherever we journey in the interim with the Lord is just as important as the final destination.

We are being groomed in leadership through servanthood. We are being prepared for ministry through patience and love for one another. Faithfulness and character are being built, and trust is being established.

The Lord is patiently preparing our hearts to steward the mysteries of God faithfully.

During this period of waiting, it would be wise to consider time as our friend and not as our enemy. We must embrace this process because it is God's wisdom for our longevity. God doesn't want to send us out prematurely, only to cave under pressure. He would rather invest in us for the long term.

Jesus was in preparation for 30 years, for a 3 ½ year public ministry. The preparation time far exceeded the length of His public exposure. And due to the depth of the preparation in His life, the impact He made is still felt today.

Imagine If He had prepared for three years, and ministered for thirty. We can't picture it, can we?

All things considered, the timing of the Lord is perfect. He's mercifully keeping us from pride. Undergoing an additional year of preparation will enable you to withstand conceit in the years to follow. In His wisdom, He knows when you're ready.

What good would it be if He were to send you out a year premature, only to burn out in five? Wouldn't you rather be sent in the fullness of His timing, and endure until the end? He knows what He's doing... trust Him. He's working the precious commodity of patience in your life. Just hold on! You are where every child of God has been before. God is faithful; He will surely perfect that which concerns you.

> *"Being confident of this very thing, that he which hath begun a good work in you will perform it until the day of Jesus Christ." (Philippians 1:6)*

Wilderness

When reading Deuteronomy 8 in the light of Christ, we see the heart of God more perfectly as He elaborates on the wilderness period:

> *"And thou shalt remember all the way which the Lord thy God led thee these forty years in the wilderness, to humble thee, and to prove thee, to know what was in thine heart, whether thou wouldest keep his commandments, or no. And he humbled thee, and suffered thee to hunger, and fed thee with manna, which thou knewest not, neither did thy fathers know; that he might make thee know that man doth not live by bread only, but by every word that proceedeth out of the mouth of the Lord doth man live." (Deuteronomy 8:2, 3)*

And he humbled thee... God used this time to humble the children of Israel. You may think, *"Weren't they humbled by Pharoah? They were slaves in poverty!"* Truth be told, they came into the wilderness full of pride! True humility is dependence upon God; It is to rely and depend on God's word.

The pride in the children of Israel's hearts arose when they rejected God's ways in the desert. Every time they were faced with a decision to turn to God, they turned to Egypt.

The wilderness births trust in God or aborts hope. The choice is ours.

This is our training ground. This is the time of decisiveness. We will either rely on His manna and trust His intentions, or we're going to revert to Egypt.

"Thou shalt also consider in thine heart, that, as a man chasteneth his son, so the Lord thy God chasteneth thee." (Deuteronomy 8:5)

What kind of father wouldn't correct his children? A good father will do everything he can to prepare his children for a successful life. So much more, our Father! The wilderness, or preparation process, is as a boot camp where our Father equips us for success in His kingdom.

We were slaves, but now we're sons and daughters; we've come in as civilians, but leave as soldiers. We are equipped in belief as our manner of warfare. If we are to be ambassadors of Christ, we ought to know how our Father thinks, speaks, dresses, and acts.

"...and that he might prove thee, to do thee good at thy latter end." (Deuteronomy 8:16)

To do you good in the end... The Lord is taking the time and proving us now, so we don't quickly faint later.

When Paul received Christ, he spent three years in the deserts alone:

*"But when it pleased God, who separated me from my mother's womb, and called me by his grace, **To reveal his Son in me**, that I might preach him among the heathen; immediately I conferred not with flesh and blood: Neither went I up to Jerusalem to them which were apostles before me; but I went into Arabia, and returned again unto Damascus. **Then after three years**…" (Galatians 1:15-18) (emphasis mine)*

He spent three years in the desert to have Jesus revealed in Him! This is the purpose of our time in the wilderness. Not to murmur and complain, and altogether miss the promised land, not to wander in darkness and sorrow: but a time of becoming like Jesus.

"Then fourteen years after I went up again to Jerusalem with Barnabas, and took Titus with me also. And I went up by revelation…" (Galatians 2:1)

A revelation of Jesus is what the Father has in mind.
How about John the Baptist?

"And the child grew, and waxed strong in spirit, and was in the deserts till the day of his shewing unto Israel." (Luke 1:80)

John was in the desert for most of his life. The wilderness period caused him to grow strong in the spirit! Not as the children of Israel who remained in Egypt in their hearts, John the Baptist chose to learn of God's ways in his time of preparation.

He ate locusts and wild honey, wore camel's hair with a leather girdle, abstained from alcohol, and was a Nazarite preacher of righteousness. He must have been an intense man, wouldn't you think?

David is another example:

"And it came to pass, when the evil spirit from God was upon Saul, that David took a harp, and played with his hand: so Saul was refreshed, and was well, and the evil spirit departed from him." (1st Samuel 16:23)

David had been playing the harp and worshipping God from a boy. When he played before Saul, he wasn't playing before Saul at all... he was playing before the Lord. He was a shepherd and spent his time in the wilderness, yet he was anointed king as a teenager. He was a king in the wilderness!

"And David said unto Saul, Thy servant kept his father's sheep, and there came a lion, and a bear, and took a lamb out of the flock...and when he arose against me, I caught him by his beard, and smote him, and slew him." (1st Samuel 17:34, 35)

He was in preparation long before he ever played for Saul, or stood before Goliath. He had already faced a lion and a bear! His worship and trust in the Lord enabled him to prosper before Goliath. David prevailed because of his time alone with God. When the time came to sit on the throne, he then had the godly character required to uphold justice, mercy, and truth.

Jesus. Our wonderful Jesus, the most prepared of all. The perfect representation of One who would wholly follow in His Father's footsteps. He spent 33 ½ years of His life in complete trust, obedience and surrender. His 40-day wilderness period wasn't the time of His preparation. His whole life was.

When the enemy came to Jesus with temptation, He was already convinced of His identity as a Son. This was Him spying out the land and disregarding the giants. This was the 40-day and night flood of Noah while remaining calm in the ark. This was Him declaring scripture from Deuteronomy for the hundred-millionth time. This was Him saying yes to who He already knew He was. This was the open show, after having practiced behind the scenes for thirty years.

The wilderness of Jesus was the confirmation of His public ministry, but no one saw it except His Father. Despising the temptation in the wilderness was not the enablement to His success. It was knowing He was God's beloved Son.

We all have a preparation time set apart by God because we are His beloved sons and daughters. Our whole life is that of preparation, but there are goals met, and pinnacles reached along the way. There is a vital process before we step out, and there are processes of equal importance throughout the journey.

Bear this always in mind: God has not promised us the wilderness; He has promised us an inheritance. What God spoke will surely come to pass in our lives. Preparation time is never wasted time. Without the preparation, we'll miss out on all that God has for us.

"…and that he might prove thee, to do thee good at thy latter end."
Deuteronomy 8:16

What child doesn't want to be like their father when they grow up? They try on his clothes, and they step into his shoes. They follow his patterns, trying to sound and act like him. They are little versions of their father. That's who we are as Christians. We are *little Christs'*. Our preparation time is getting to know our Father. He is overjoyed when we try on His clothes and step into His shoes.

Now, this is an example of what our preparation time should *not* be like:

"And they said unto Moses, Because there were no graves in Egypt, hast thou taken us away to die in the wilderness? wherefore hast thou dealt thus with us, to carry us forth out of Egypt? Is not this the word that we did tell thee in Egypt, saying, Let us alone, that we may serve the Egyptians? For it had been better for us to serve the Egyptians, than that we should die in the wilderness." (Exodus 14:11, 12)

Nothing but murmuring and complaining. Not one mention of God's goodness and how He delivered them from bondage. They gave place to temptation in the wilderness because they weren't waiting on God. They weren't diligently keeping their hearts.

Here is a successful response to temptation, and our ultimate example:

"But he answered and said, It is written, Man shall not live by bread alone, but by every word that proceedeth out of the mouth of God." (Matthew 4:4)

Jesus' response to temptation is the only thing to consider: *It is written.* Likewise, we need to respond to temptation by declaring and focusing on the word, which is Jesus. As we wait on God, it's vital that we remain encouraged in our wildernesses, and to come out of them empowered. Jesus came out of His wilderness in power, and so should we.

Lord, Save Me!

One of the most effective prayers of mine is a simple yet powerful declaration: *"Lord, save me."*

As soon as I sense an attack or resistance, I stand my ground, submit to the Lord, and invite His strength into my life by proclaiming, *"Lord, save me!"*

*"For whosoever shall call upon the name of the Lord shall be **saved**." (Romans 10:13) (emphasis mine)*

When you study the word *saved* here, it is translated from the Greek word, *sozo,* which means: *keep safe or sound, rescue from danger, deliver, protect, or make whole.* This verse is not implied for our initial encounter with the Lord upon salvation only, but an ongoing and continuous declaration. I have found that wisdom would call for us to rely on His strength constantly. His strength is made perfect in our weaknesses.

"I can do all things through Christ which strengtheneth me." (Philippians 4:13)

Here is wisdom: consider yourself weak in the flesh and always rely on the strength of the Lord. You can do all things… *through Christ…* Who gives you the strength. Consider this passage found in second Corinthians:

"For though he was crucified through weakness, yet he liveth by the power of God. For we also are weak in him, but we shall live with him by the power of God toward you." (2nd Corinthians 13:4)

Our flesh is weak, but His Spirit is strong in us! To be crucified with Christ is to live in His resurrection power.

*"Finally, my brethren, be strong in the Lord, and in the **power of his might**." (Ephesians 6:10) (emphasis mine)*

Consider Samson. In the natural, he was the strongest man that ever lived. Nevertheless, he succumbed to temptation. Resisting temptation is not tied to your strength or will in the flesh, but in your relationship with God. Being a Nazarite, Samson's strength was tied to the *covenant* he had with God Almighty.

Had Samson followed this principle found in the book of James, his story may have ended differently:

"Submit yourselves therefore to God. Resist the devil, and he will flee from you." (James 4:7)

Notice how the scripture says to submit to God first. It doesn't say, *"Resist the devil and submit yourself to God..."* This is key. Your submission to God *brings* resistance to the enemy, not the other way around.

Fighting temptation in your own strength will be as Samson resisting Delilah. You cannot entertain Delilah and easily walk away. We need to flee the scene as Joseph did from Potiphar's wife:

"Flee also youthful lusts..." (2nd Timothy 2:22)

Recognizing that you always need the strength of Christ is great wisdom! This will spare you from being bound by the enemy and having your joy stripped away. Don't be as Samson, trusting in your own strength; be wise like Joseph, and run away.

My "running away" is really running straight to God in the first place. If I'm trying to resist the devil in my own power, I'll fall, but if I submit to God, the devil has no chance! I believe most Christians are missing the first part of this verse when dealing with the tempter. Most believers are trying to resist the devil in order to submit to God. However, this strategy will prove to be fruitless.

The perspective I have of this verse is inviting Jesus into the midst of the temptation by fleeing to Him and saying, *"Lord, save me! Deliver and protect me! Rescue me!"* This approach will allow the strength of God to overcome the enemy's attack. The enemy will flee from you as you flee to God.

Now, you may be able to withstand a few attacks in your own strength. Sure, you may win a few battles, but the enemy knows you are fighting apart from the Lord. He'll just take a few more demons along with him in his next attack! However, if you invite Almighty God into the fight, he'll surely reconsider.

When reading James' admonition in the proper context, we are left with a greater understanding of our full dependency on the strength of Jesus Christ. Adopting this approach over time will cause faith and patience to have her perfect work. You'll soon find confidence relying on His strength, rather than resisting in your own.

The enemy will bring temptation through lust and haste, to have you settle for what you want now, rather than what you'd want most in the future. Wait on God in this wisdom, and you'll be left with contentment, rather than regret.

Pure Gold

When Jesus was tempted in the wilderness, the enemy came after His identity. Imagine Jesus as a 100% pure gold bar. There is no impurity in Him! There's no dross, nor imperfection. If I were to give such a gold bar to a jeweler and say: *"Test this, please. See if it's pure."*

After a thorough inspection, that jeweler would hand it back, and say: *"I find no impurity in it."*

This is what Pilate said concerning Jesus: "*I find no fault in Him…*" (Luke 23:4).

Upon the devil's inspection of Jesus, he could only try to make Him *question* His purity. However, a pure gold bar is a pure gold bar. Jesus didn't fall for it. Now, this is exactly what the enemy tries to do with us!

"Has God said you're forgiven? Has God said you're His son? Do you think God really loves someone like you? Has God called you here? *Hath God said?"*

We can't fall for this either! The enemy can only try to detract our focus from Jesus and have us identify with our past. Nevertheless, as He is, so are we. We need to be assured of the pure gold bars that our Father has made us through Christ.

Jesus responded with the word: "It is written." It is *sure*. We ought to follow Jesus' example alone. The word is *always* our response to temptation, never how we feel. Right before this temptation, the Father said:

"…This is my beloved Son, in whom I am well pleased." (Matthew 3:17)

Jesus didn't entertain any other word spoken in contradiction to His Father. He didn't respond according to His hunger. He responded according to His identity in the word. Thank you, Jesus, for not selling your birthright for the stew of the devil.

Let's pause for a moment while in the wilderness, and fast-forward into the promised land ahead. We'll spy out the land for ourselves before we ever move in. In fact, this is what we do each time we read of God's promises in the first place. Every time we meditate on His word, we're spying out the land of our inheritance.

Reading this account in the right perspective reveals *how* the giants are waiting for us on the other side. Rahab's report will provide a great perspective for us while in preparation. This will ground us in hope while waiting, and cause faith to rise to the occasion. If we catch a glimpse of the enemy's camp while in the wilderness, the giants won't stand a chance upon our arrival.

We Shall Believe The Report Of The Lord

"And she said unto the men, I know that the LORD hath given you the land, and that your terror is fallen upon us, and that all the inhabitants of the land faint because of you." (Joshua 2:9)

Moses sent twelve men into Canaan to spy out the land and bring back a report. All twelve of them came back having seen the same things, but only two saw the promised land differently: Joshua the son of Nun, from the tribe of Ephraim; and Caleb the son of Jephunneh, from the tribe of Judah. These would be the only two men of the first generation (who originally exited Egypt) that would enter the promised land.

Upon the spies return, the ten only spoke of what they saw, not of what God said. The following passages reveal the gravity of sin in the unbelief brought back into camp. For this cause, they all missed the promised land:

"And they told him, and said, We came unto the land whither thou sentest us, and surely it floweth with milk and honey; and this is the fruit of it. Nevertheless the people be strong that dwell in the land, and the cities are walled, and very great: and moreover we saw the children of Anak there. The Amalekites dwell in the land of the south: and the Hittites, and the Jebusites, and the Amorites, dwell in the mountains: and the Canaanites dwell by the sea, and by the coast of Jordan." (Numbers 13:27-29)

There was only one sentence in this account, mentioning the surety of God's report, and the rest of their speech was full of doubt and fear. They then go on to explain in greater detail how they cannot overtake the giants!

"But the men that went up with him said, We be not able to go up against the people; for they are stronger than we. And they brought up an evil report of the land which they had searched unto the children of Israel, saying, The land, through which we have gone to search it, is a land that eateth up the inhabitants thereof; and all the people that we saw in it are men of a great stature. And there we saw the giants, the sons of Anak, which come of the giants: and we were in our own sight as grasshoppers, and so we were in their sight." (Numbers 13:31-33)

Upon hearing this slanderous report, the congregation became polluted. As waters become polluted, so did all the children of Israel through unbelief. What a disgrace... how could they have so quickly forgotten what God had done in Egypt?

Beyond any shadow of a doubt, the Lord obliterated the land. From the Nile, and all water sources being turned into blood, to the frogs and the lice. From the swarms of flies to the widespread destruction of their livestock. From the boils, the fiery hail, and the locusts, to the tangible darkness that enveloped them, to the death angel, then killing all of Egypt's firstborn sons and animals.

If this wasn't enough to have convinced you against natural circumstances, the whole Red Sea stood up like a wall! Not to mention, a pillar of fire and a cloud led them through on dry ground.

Finally, as Moses stretched forth his staff, the Lord collapsed the sea upon Pharaoh and his army, drowning every last one of them.

Considering the infinite power of God, how could these tiny giants stand a chance? How could the spies be so confident in their inability, rather than in *His* ability? Even worse, they became prophets for the enemy; they spewed forth their doubt and fear on everybody else.

Through God's deliverance, the Israelites exited Egypt unscathed; what should have changed concerning their deliverance from the giants? The Lord Himself *promised* that He would give them the land! He promised this before He delivered the children out of Egypt. In fact, God promised deliverance from Egypt before they were ever enslaved.

They needed only to believe.

I love the response from Joshua and Caleb. They saw the land quite differently.

"And Caleb stilled the people before Moses, and said, Let us go up at once, and possess it; for we are well able to overcome it...Only rebel not ye against the Lord, neither fear ye the people of the land; for they are bread for us: their defence is departed from them, and the Lord is with us: fear them not." (Numbers 13:30, 14:9)

Keep in mind, all twelve spies saw the same things in Canaan. Nevertheless, Joshua and Caleb saw things differently because they *heard* God's report differently.

I've heard it said how the enemy of vision is sight. Often, what we see in the natural will try to take preeminence over what we see in our hearts, which is vision. Vision comes from a place within, and must be guarded, and anchored, in hope. The whole Christian faith is predicated on the reality of the substance of things that are *not* seen! This is faith, and faith pleases God. We cannot determine if God's report is true by looking at the circumstances.

Here's an example:

"You know, the Lord must not have called me here... everything seems to be going the other way! Surely, I must have missed it. He must be calling me somewhere else."

One thing I've realized is when things get difficult, it often proves God's calling! Jesus was met with persecution *everywhere* He went.

Paul was given an effectual door opening when writing to the church at Corinth but said there were many adversaries (1st Corinthians 16:9).

Another open door for Paul and Silas was through the vision of a man from Macedonia, saying, "help us" (Acts 16:9). Ironically, they were soon beaten and delivered to prison, after ministering deliverance to others.

These men had an important decision to make while in prison: begin to question if God had truly called them there... or praise Him for the fact that He did, regardless of how they felt. Likewise, we must choose to remember the open door from the Lord when considering our circumstances. This way, we won't allow the present situation to ever distort what God had spoken first.

We must look back and remember the clear word from God when we find ourselves in uncertainty. We should be quick to remind ourselves:

"I *know* the Lord spoke to me; I *know* He called me here. As for what I am coming up against, this too shall pass. I will not allow this circumstance to determine what God has said. Yes, God *has* said."

What the enemy wants is for you to believe that you missed God from the beginning. He does this by bringing attention to the present difficulty! He wants to sow a seed of doubt. This is his only tactic!

"Hath God said?"

If he can make you believe something other than what God has said, he can take you out. He is a liar and the father of it. What the Lord desires for us when we're uncertain is to become still, so not to make a hasty and emotional decision.

Touching back on the Macedonian account, when Paul and Silas began to praise God, the whole prison was shaken by an earthquake. Each door swung open, and the jail keeper and his family were saved shortly thereafter! The jailer then went on to wash their backs from the beatings. They were soon released and comforted by the brethren before departing from the city. What a testimony!

This relates to us more than we may think. When Paul and Silas obeyed the leading of the Lord, they saw fruit immediately… only to be beaten and imprisoned shortly after. For us, if we only take into consideration the persecution for the word's sake, we may begin to question if the opened door was God to begin with. We could start to waiver if we only consider the trial.

This account provides great insight for us. If Paul and Silas had given a poor testimony while incarcerated, they would have missed a tremendous opportunity to witness to those in prison. They were able to effectively minister through God's open door despite the fact it was incredibly difficult.

Something is compelling about a person who is subjected to the fires of life like everybody else, but not consumed. There's an attraction from the Lord given to those around them. A peace this world cannot offer.

They consider: *"Why are they so at rest right now; how can this be?"*

This becomes an open door for you to minister to those imprisoned around you!

Moses was attracted to the burning bush that wasn't consumed. God then spoke to him as he approached. This encounter changed his entire life! We need to be as the bush that the fires of life cannot consume to those around us. This will give place for God to speak through us when they take notice.

Paul and Silas could have been consumed along with those in jail. Instead, they released the power of the Lord to those in need. They may have been temporarily shackled, but they were *already* free. This opened the door of freedom to all those around them. They didn't allow the closed door of circumstance to dictate the open door of the Lord.

Bearing this in mind, the Lord has opened the door for us into the promised land. Whatever lays wait on the other side is either for us or against us. It is either in our way or helps along the way. Either way, God is for us... so what can be against us?

Rahab's Report

"As soon as we heard these things..."

When Joshua had the chance to search out the land, he sent two spies instead of twelve. I don't think he wanted to take any chances this time. It didn't go so well for him and Caleb 40 years prior! Two spies came back, believing God's report upon the initial sending, and Joshua wanted to achieve the same results.

In speculation, I imagine he sent the two most faithful men in the camp to spy out the land. I believe these men already agreed with God's report before they ever stepped foot into Canaan. They were just going in to pave the way.

Upon entering, the men lodged at Rahab's house. What she said to them has shaped the way I consider the whole account.

"And she said unto the men, I know that the Lord hath given you the land, and that your terror is fallen upon us, and that all the inhabitants of the land faint because of you. For we have heard how the Lord dried up the water of the Red sea for you, when ye came out of Egypt; and what ye did unto the two kings of the Amorites, that were on the other side Jordan, Sihon and Og, whom ye utterly destroyed. And as soon as we had heard these things, our hearts did melt, neither did there remain any more courage in any man, because of you: for the Lord your God, he is God in heaven above, and in earth beneath." (Joshua 2:9-11)

If you consider the implications of this statement, you begin to realize the magnitude of the children of Israel's unbelief.

Rahab said:

"We have heard how the Lord dried up the Red Sea (*which at that point was 40 years prior*) and how the two kings were destroyed (*which was right before their entrance into Canaan*); and as soon as we heard it, our hearts melted, and we had no more courage within us to fight."

This means: the children of Israel were afraid of the giants for the forty years they wandered the wilderness... but on the other side, the giants were afraid of them!

The giants wandered around Canaan with a forty-year death sentence, thinking that at any moment, the children of Israel were going to come in and wipe them out.

When the enemy hears about the Lord destroying the land of Egypt, drying up the Red Sea in our life, and cutting off the way back, his heart utterly melts for fear and dread of us. There is no more courage within him to fight. That's why we must believe the Lord before we ever step foot into our promise because He's already paved the way!

Meditating on God's promises will enable us to withstand whatever giants lay ahead.

Now, the children of Israel didn't need to know that the giants were afraid of them; they only needed to take God at His word. They would have soon realized upon arrival that the giants were *already* subdued by the hand of the Lord. For this reason, the Lord was greatly displeased with the first generation. They missed out on all of God's goodness because they were crippled with fear.

Now that we see what we're up against, and how the Lord has already subdued our enemies, we can stop wandering the wilderness in fear. We can value the wilderness as a time of meditating on God's word, rather than meditating in doubt and unbelief.

This is our time of preparation. We are following in our Father's footsteps right into our promise. It's learning of who we are by getting to know who He is. Catching a glimpse of Jesus will change the perspective of our future. We will see that He's not setting us up to face the towering giants, but how He's already cut the legs out from underneath them.

The giants are waiting on the other side afraid of us.

Part two of this chapter will discuss how and why the Lord implemented the law. It was for a time and purpose, and it's of the utmost importance to understand its intent. Moses was unable to enter the promised land of God because of the law. If Moses, being a friend of God, couldn't enter in because of the law… who can?

Part Two: Wilderness

The Law

Upon driving home one day, the Lord showed me a glimpse of what it was like to live under the law.

As the traffic light turned green, I began to head east on Highway 24. I quickly gained speed down the winding hill and found myself going 55mph in a 45mph zone. I realized I was going that fast in the first place after seeing a sheriff parked on the shoulder.

I remember praying, *"Lord, have mercy,"* as I slowed down to the speed limit. Glancing in my rearview mirror in angst, my prayer was answered: the sheriff stayed in his place. Thank God!

Interestingly, in the five years I lived in Colorado, I never saw a police officer in that same spot again.

As soon as I passed the sheriff, the Lord spoke to me:

"Son, if you were going the speed limit, you would have justified yourself by the law..."

"Wow, that's interesting," I remember thinking to myself... but He wasn't finished speaking:

"...but you would have been blinded to the fact that you weren't wearing your seat belt."

Wow, again...

Truly, I had no intention of trying to "spiritualize" this encounter with the sheriff or try and think of what may have come from it. I wasn't considering the law; I wasn't thinking about grace. I was just relieved I didn't get a speeding ticket!

After the Lord spoke, I began to see the significance of what He had revealed. The Bible says:

"For whosoever shall keep the whole law, and yet offend in one point, he is guilty of all. For He that said, Do not commit adultery, said also, Do not kill. Now if thou commit no adultery, yet if thou kill, thou art become a transgressor of the law." (James 2:10, 11)

The Jews that were living under the law were justifying themselves by what they were keeping but were always blind to something they weren't. We know this:

"As it is written, There is none righteous, no, not one." (Romans 3:10)

"For there is not a just man upon earth, that doeth good, and sinneth not." (Ecclesiastes 7:20)

There isn't anyone, besides Jesus Christ, who could perfectly keep, and fulfill the law. Someone who is justifying themselves by the law they keep would parallel this example of the sheriff on the highway. If I were going the speed limit, I would have been justified, but I wasn't wearing my seat belt; therefore, I was a transgressor of the whole thing.

Purposed Law

"Wherefore then serveth the law?..." (Galatians 3:19)

Now, had I been going the speed limit and following the law, that sheriff would never have pulled me over and said: *"Good evening, sir. I'm pulling you over today to compliment you on your impeccable driving. The way you signaled before pulling into that lane, thumbs up, that was textbook. Also, the town of Woodland Park thanks you for going the speed limit, and for your care and concern on the road. Great job! Please, keep up the good work!"*

This would never happen! Why? The law is not in place to commend you. It's there to condemn you. If there are 99 things you have done right on the road while driving and you do one thing wrong: behold, the flashing lights in your rearview mirror. The police are not parked on the highway looking for what's right, but what's wrong.

We must have a good understanding of the law and its purpose:

*"Knowing this, that **the law is not made for a righteous man**, but for the lawless and disobedient, for the ungodly and for sinners, for unholy and profane..." (1st Timothy 1:9) (emphasis mine)*

The Lord never intended His people to live under the law. It was meant to preserve them up until Jesus.

"Wherefore then serveth the law? It was added because of transgressions, till the seed should come to whom the promise was made; and it was ordained by angels in the hand of a mediator... But before faith came, we were kept under the law, shut up unto the faith which should afterwards be revealed. Wherefore the law was our schoolmaster to bring us unto Christ, that we might be justified by faith. But after that faith is come, we are no longer under a schoolmaster." (Galatians 3:19, 23-25)

Up until the law was enacted, God was dealing with His people through mercy and grace, which are two things foreign to the law. The law is unmerciful and unbending.

Let me be clear as to set the tone throughout these next few paragraphs: the law was not made for the righteous. It is not meant to be preached in the church today for the benefit of His body, nor was it meant to perfect us. Paul calls it the ministration of condemnation (2nd Corinthians 3:9). He also rebukes the church in Galatia for their desire to go back to it. In fact, most of his writings focus on the importance of following the righteousness of faith, and to not be yoked again unto bondage.

Now, you may be reading this with a good understanding of the detriment of legalism already, and I would say amen unto you; this was not revealed to you by man, but God. Be that as it may, many in the body of Christ are under condemnation and fear because of the ministration of the law.

It may not be as blatant as the recital of the ten commandments each week, or the handwashing, sabbath day journeys, and ritual ceremonies performed, but rather the subtle, self-focus preaching, that causes you to take your eyes off Jesus.

It's the mindset of confessing all your sins before bed or the fear of losing your salvation. It is re-dedicating your life at the altar in hopes to finally conquer your shortcomings. It is walking away after church introspectively, with the incessant need to "do better." It's being told: *"Thou shalt not!"*

Rather than: *"It is finished."*

The steady diet of legalism will have you focusing on your faults, rather than on His perfection.

This is a spiritual matter we're discussing here, and I pray through the course of this book there is a freedom revealed by the Holy Ghost. Consider what Romans says about it, and afterward, we can elaborate:

"For I was alive without the law once: but when the commandment came, sin revived, and I died. And the commandment, which was ordained to life, I found to be unto death. For sin, taking occasion by the commandment, deceived me, and by it slew me. Wherefore the law is holy, and the commandment holy, and just, and good. Was then that which is good made death unto me? God forbid. But sin, that it might appear sin, working death in me by that which is good; that sin by the commandment might become exceeding sinful." (Romans 7:9-13)

See how Paul says: *"I was alive without the law once."*

Sin was present since the fall of man but was never dealt with at the root. The law was given to shine a light on the root, not pull it up.

Therein lies the frustration of Paul as he continues to write of his confliction:

"For I know that in me (that is, in my flesh,) dwelleth no good thing: for to will is present with me; but how to perform that which is good I find not. For the good that I would I do not: but the evil which I would not, that I do...O wretched man that I am! who shall deliver me from the body of this death? I thank God through Jesus Christ our Lord. So then with the mind I myself serve the law of God, but with the flesh the law of sin." (Romans 7:18-19, 24-25)

The righteousness of the law demands perfection; the holiness of the law demands justice. However, the law demands a change of action without providing the instruction on *how* to do it. We needed a change of nature first!

When an immoral man is placed before the holiness of the law, condemnation is the only result. We stood no chance against the law. The conflict was the desire to do what was right, with the predisposition of doing what was wrong.

See, the law wasn't the cure for the disease of sin. It was its uncovering. It was the magnet that caused all the metal to surface; it was the light in the darkness that drew all the moths.

"For the law was given by Moses, but grace and truth came by Jesus Christ." (John 1:17)

The law was truth without grace. What the law could not do, Jesus would exemplify. The law would be swallowed up in victory through His fierce love for us. *Demonstrated* love. Jesus, through interaction and instruction, would be what we were missing: Relationship.

"That which was from the beginning, which we have heard, which we have seen with our eyes, which we have looked upon, and our hands have handled, of the Word of Life." (1st John 1:1)

"And the Word was made flesh, and dwelt among us, (and we beheld his glory, the glory as of the only begotten of the Father,) full of grace and truth." (John 1:14)

Emmanuel: God with us! The word was made flesh, not written upon a stone. The law was impersonal and unsympathetic; Jesus moved with compassion. The law was unmovable and incapable of intimacy; Jesus was full of grace and truth. Not as the law, which was only truth: but truth *and* grace.

Ah, grace. What wonderful grace! The grace that would enable change. This relationship would change everything, and His grace is what we were missing!

Now that we have briefly discussed the law's purpose let's discuss Moses for a moment. Moses will tie a few loose ends together in our pursuit of ministering righteousness. We'll see why he missed the promised land, and why Joshua led the charge instead.

Speak Unto This Rock

The Lord commanded Moses to speak to the rock, which would give the assembly water:

> *"Take the rod, and gather thou the assembly together, thou, and Aaron thy brother, and speak ye unto the rock before their eyes; and it shall give forth his water, and thou shalt bring forth to them the water out of the rock..." (Numbers 20:8)*

However, Moses disobeyed and struck the rock twice instead:

> *"And Moses took the rod from before the Lord, as he commanded him. And Moses and Aaron gathered the congregation together before the rock, and he said unto them, Hear now, ye rebels; must we fetch you water out of this rock? And Moses lifted up his hand, and with his rod he smote the rock twice: and the water came out abundantly, and the congregation drank, and their beasts also. And the Lord spake unto Moses and Aaron, Because ye believed me not, to sanctify me in the eyes of the children of Israel, therefore ye shall not bring this congregation into the land which I have given them." (Numbers 20:9-12)*

The account of Moses striking the rock instead of speaking to it may leave us astonished at the severity of the punishment he received:

"And the Lord spake unto Moses that selfsame day, saying, Get thee up into this mountain Abarim, unto mount Nebo, which is in the land of Moab, that is over against Jericho; and behold the land of Canaan, which I give unto the children of Israel for a possession: And die in the mount whither thou goest up, and be gathered unto thy people; as Aaron thy brother died in mount Hor, and was gathered unto his people: Because ye trespassed against me among the children of Israel at the waters of Meribah-Kadesh, in the wilderness of Zin; because ye sanctified me not in the midst of the children of Israel. Yet thou shalt see the land before thee; but thou shalt not go thither unto the land which I give the children of Israel." (Deuteronomy 32:48-52)

I remember thinking: *"Lord, the punishment doesn't seem to fit the crime."*

What could be the reason for such a harsh consequence?

Consider Moses' life: He was forty years in Egypt and gave up all the power and glory to follow God. He then spent the next forty years in the backside of a desert caring for sheep. At eighty, he stood before Pharaoh and delivered the children of Israel out of Egypt... into yet another desert! There, he spent the remaining forty years of his life serving God and shepherding a rebellious congregation, only to seemingly miss it all and die before entering the promised land.

This was Moses, the friend of God! The one who spoke with Him face, to Face! Wasn't this Moses, the meekest man on earth? Wasn't this the one who interceded for the people (on multiple occasions), and changed God's mind towards their destruction? This was God's man!

This account always left me wondering. *Why wasn't Moses allowed in?*

Truly, if Moses wasn't allowed in, who was? When I sought the Lord on this, He revealed to me the reason he *couldn't* enter.

Moses was undoubtedly a friend and servant of God, but he also represented the law. There was no mercy for Moses because there is no mercy in the law. Moses delivered the law; therefore, he was judged by it. If you live by the sword you shall also die by it. Moses did everything right, all to miss the promised land for the one thing he did wrong.

"For whosoever shall keep the whole law, and yet offend in one point, he is guilty of all." (James 2:10)

Moses' judgment was set the moment he struck the rock. As we continue to read, we can see Moses asking God for mercy:

"And I besought the Lord at that time, saying, O Lord God, thou hast begun to shew thy servant thy greatness, and thy mighty hand: for what God is there in heaven or in earth, that can do according to thy works, and according to thy might? I pray thee, let me go over, and see the good land that is beyond Jordan, that goodly mountain, and Lebanon. But the Lord was wroth with me for your sakes, and would not hear me: and the Lord said unto me, Let it suffice thee; speak no more unto me of this matter. Get thee up into the top of Pisgah, and lift up thine eyes westward, and northward, and southward, and eastward, and behold it with thine eyes: for thou shalt not go over this Jordan. But charge Joshua, and encourage him, and strengthen him: for he shall go over before this people, and he shall cause them to inherit the land which thou shalt see." (Deuteronomy 3:23-28)

Doesn't this sound like a similar decree from God to Abraham?

"And the Lord said unto Abram, after that Lot was separated from him, Lift up now thine eyes, and look from the place where thou art northward, and southward, and eastward, and westward: For all the land which thou seest, to thee will I give it, and to thy seed for ever." (Genesis 13:14, 15)

When God told Moses to look in all four directions, He said *thou shalt not*; there was no mercy. But when God told Abraham to look in all four directions, He said *you shall have it!* The inheritance was given to Abraham by faith, not by the works of the law.

Who then was able to enter in? Joshua and Caleb; grace and truth.

*"But my servant Caleb, **because he had another spirit with him**, and hath followed me fully, him will I bring into the land whereinto he went; and his seed shall possess it." (Numbers 14:24) (emphasis mine)*

Joshua is another name for Jesus or Yeshua. Caleb believed God and went with "another" spirit: *Jesus*. Caleb entered the promised land with Jesus! Their inheritance was that of faith righteousness, not the righteousness of the law.

Naturally speaking, if you live for the righteousness of the law, like Moses, you will always fall short.

"Christ is become of no effect unto you, whosoever of you are justified by the law; ye are fallen from grace." (Galatians 5:4)

The righteousness the law has to offer will only bring you as far as the mountaintop to *see* the promised land, but you can never enter in. It requires a death. Jesus was going to be the one who died upon the mountaintop for us to enter in through *His* righteousness!

We can never enter God's rest in our own strength. Notice the scripture said Moses was full of strength with perfect eyesight at 120 years old:

> *"And Moses was an hundred and twenty years old when he died: his eye was not dim, nor his natural force abated." (Deuteronomy 34:7)*

Our natural force is not enough. The flesh cannot inherit! It would require a supernatural force.

> *"And seeing one of them suffer wrong, he defended him, and avenged him that was oppressed, and smote the Egyptian: For he supposed his brethren would have understood how that God by his hand would deliver them: but they understood not." (Acts 7:24, 25)*

It's not by our force or might! Moses buried one Egyptian in the sand by his own hand, but God buried all of Pharaoh's army in the Red Sea by His.

In hindsight, the severity of Moses' punishment was perfect. If he was able to enter in by his own strength and righteousness, or if he deserved it more than somebody else, Jesus would have died in vain.

Furthermore, the law never loses its force, nor its focus. Its vision is clear! Like Moses never lost his strength, neither does the law. He died in perfect shape but missed out on the promise.

Now, what does the Bible say the strength of sin is?

> *"The sting of death is sin; and the strength of sin is the law." (1st Corinthians 15:56)*

The definition of sin is to *miss the mark*. The ministration of the law will cause us to miss the mark like Moses! Therefore, we are to minister grace to the hearers (Ephesians 4:29). Ministering the law to the body will only strengthen sin.

> *"Moreover the law entered, that the offence might abound. But where sin abounded, grace did much more abound." (Romans 5:20)*

Grace is stronger! Jesus fulfilled the law, and He *is* the grace of God. When Jesus ministers to us, he now encourages the righteousness within. The way to perfect the body is to minister grace, which builds up, not to establish the law which tears down. The law will condemn, but grace will commend.

The sum of the whole matter is this: Love. We fulfill the whole law by accepting Jesus' righteousness and walking in love.

"For all the law is fulfilled in one word, even in this; Thou shalt love thy neighbor as thyself." (Galatians 5:14)

"Owe no man any thing, but to love one another: for he that loveth another hath fulfilled the law. For this, Thou shalt not commit adultery, Thou shalt not kill, Thou shalt not steal, Thou shalt not bear false witness, Thou shalt not covet; and if there be any other commandment, it is briefly comprehended in this saying, namely, Thou shalt love thy neighbor as thyself. Love worketh no ill to his neighbor: therefore love is the fulfilling of the law." (Romans 13:8-10)

Do you know what the opposite of love is? Most people think it would be hate; however, hate is not the opposite of love, fear is.

"There is no fear in love; but perfect love casteth out fear: because fear hath torment. He that feareth is not made perfect in love." (1st John 4:18)

It was a fearful thing when the law was given:

"And it came to pass on the third day in the morning, that there were thunders and lightnings, and a thick cloud upon the mount, and the voice of the trumpet exceeding loud; so that all the people that was in the camp trembled." (Exodus 19:16)

The camp trembled! Mount Sinai violently quaked and smoked like a furnace, as the Lord descended in fire upon it. If anyone were to touch the mountain, they would have been killed! God warned how if they were so much to gaze upon Him, they would have died!

"And they said unto Moses, Speak thou with us, and we will hear: but let not God speak with us, lest we die. And Moses said unto the people, Fear not: for God is come to prove you, and that his fear may be before your faces, that ye sin not." (Exodus 20:19-20)

The people were terrified! Moses ended with:

"That His fear may be before you that you sin not."

They were the *children* of Israel. I believe this account was written for us to understand the purpose of the law.

Children Of Men, Children Of God

When I talk about children, I am talking about natural children. They have not yet been born-again. There is a difference, obviously, between a child in the faith and a child in the natural. A child in the natural needs the firmness of the law. But a child in the faith should never be introduced to the law for their instruction. The instructor is Christ within. A "child" in the faith may be any age!

"Knowing this, that the law is not made for a righteous man, but for the lawless and disobedient..." (1st Timothy 1:9)

Righteousness is not attained later; it is given as a gift upon salvation. Therefore, the law is never to be introduced to a born-again believer because they are *already* righteous. The law does not perfect righteousness.

There is a difference between a child in the faith, a young man in the faith, and a father in the faith. Yet still, they aren't nourished up by the law to grow, but by love and grace. Your natural child may need a spanking and fear not to disobey, but a child in the faith will be nourished by the milk of God's word, and grow in grace.

"As newborn babes, desire the sincere milk of the word, that ye may grow thereby: If so be ye have tasted that the Lord is gracious." (1st Peter 2:2, 3)

"But grow in grace, and in the knowledge of our Lord and Saviour Jesus Christ. To him be glory both now and for ever. Amen." (2nd Peter 3:18)

A lot of us have been milking off the wrong cow. The true milk of God's word is love and grace, not the fear induced by the law. The meat of God's word is righteousness, which cannot be chewed by someone nourished up in the law. We must be nourished up in grace to walk in righteousness.

When rebellious, a child will obey because they have been spanked! Children cannot be reasoned with until they reach an age of understanding. You cannot explain righteousness or grace to a child. They need the rod. Until they can confess Jesus as Lord, they don't have the capability to walk in love, grace, and righteousness. They aren't capable because they don't have Jesus yet within! (Of course, a child is not spanked for every mistake, but for utter rebellion.)

Until faith comes, they are under a schoolmaster. They need to fear the Lord and not sin. The correction of the word may not always penetrate their heart through explanation, but the rod of correction penetrates quite well. Christ has not yet made them righteous; therefore, by default, they are unrighteous.

Moreover, our children are born unrighteous, which qualifies them to have the law used against them. You are either righteous, or you are not. There is no in-between.

"Foolishness is bound in the heart of a child; but the rod of correction shall drive it far from him...Withhold not correction from the child: for if thou beatest him with the rod, he shall not die. Thou shalt beat him with the rod, and shalt deliver his soul from hell." (Proverbs 22:15, 23:13, 14)

Therefore, the firmness of the law was to be their schoolmaster, and the fear of disobedience was to preserve them. Until faith came, until love came, until Jesus.

Now, when you become born-again, It's no longer an outward spank of the rod of God: it's the Bible and the inner workings of love and grace. We cannot spank a mature body of believers through fear of the law. This will stunt their growth.

The body of Christ has become malnourished due to the lack of the meat of righteousness.

"For when for the time ye ought to be teachers, ye have need that one teach you again which be the first principles of the oracles of God; and are become such as have need of milk, and not of strong meat. For every one that useth milk is unskilful in the word of righteousness: for he is a babe. But strong meat belongeth to them that are of full age, even those who by reason of use have their senses exercised to discern both good and evil." (Hebrews 5:12-14)

We were incapable of fulfilling the law because we were incapable of walking in God's love. Now that we have had our stony heart removed, and have been given a heart of flesh, we have been perfected in His love! For this cause, our new identity and nature must be the focus. Not the law, which was the instrument used in exposing our corrupted nature: but grace, which has now become our teacher.

> *"For the grace of God that bringeth salvation hath appeared unto all men, Teaching us that, denying ungodliness and worldly lusts, we should live soberly, righteously, and godly, in this present world." (Titus 2:11, 12)*

> *"As every man hath received the gift, even so, minister the same one to another, as good stewards of the manifold grace of God." (1st Peter 4:10)*

We've now approached mount Zion, and have fellowship with the living God.

> *"For ye are not come unto the mount that might be touched, and that burned with fire, nor unto blackness, and darkness, and tempest...And so terrible was the sight, that Moses said, I exceedingly fear and quake:) But ye are come unto mount Sion, and unto the city of the living God, the heavenly Jerusalem, and to an innumerable company of angels, To the general assembly and church of the firstborn, which are written in heaven, and to God the Judge of all, and to the spirits of just men made perfect." (Hebrews 12:18, 21-23)*

Through this brief discussion of the law and its purpose, we can walk away with a better understanding of its ministration.

Chapter Six

What Is This?

The mind can be fickle if not anchored in the right perspective. It's where we choose to live in our minds that will either cause contentment or dissatisfaction. The Israelites longed for the food of Egypt but forgot they were slaves. We may reminisce about our pasts also, but neglect to remember the emptiness.

As we continue to move forward in our wilderness experience, we leave more of Egypt behind. God would feed the children of Israel manna to replace the bread of Pharaoh.

Patience is being birthed, our souls are being renewed, and we can begin to see the fruits of our labor. We've come to terms that there is no way back to Egypt, and we've fully accepted the future in God's Hands. We've laid down our kneading trough's long ago, and have picked up the manna. We're in transition and have subjected our soul unto God.

There are frustrations, there are some tears, but the Lord is refining us through it all. Though there is fire involved, it causes the dross in the silver to surface. God is an all-consuming fire and wants to consume us with His love. First, however, He must purge the fear. His love is the tool of refinery.

It Is Manna

"And when the children of Israel saw it, they said one to another, It is manna: for they wist not what it was. And Moses said unto them, This is the bread which the LORD hath given you to eat." (Exodus 16:15)

When the children of Israel had first seen manna, they said, "what is it?" This is something I have come to realize when first encountering God's ways. We come across an unfamiliar path or find ourselves in trial or trouble, and we can't help but think in our minds, *what is this?*

All things considered, we've forsaken our father's house, and have left everything behind. However, we've inevitably discovered how His ways were not our own. Though we left the leaven of sin behind, the way of Egypt was more familiar. We considered the way things were… and things, well… things were *better*.

> *"We remember the fish, which we did eat in Egypt freely; the cucumbers, and the melons, and the leeks, and the onions, and the garlick."* *(Numbers 11:5)*

We could fall prey to the same train of thought as the Israelites. When times get hard, we may consider how things were, and in turn, begin to magnify our past. Through this distorted view, our soul will begin to reject what God has for us and cry out for quail.

> *"And the mixt multitude that was among them fell a lusting: and the children of Israel also wept again, and said, Who shall give us flesh to eat?…And the people spake against God, and against Moses, Wherefore have ye brought us up out of Egypt to die in the wilderness? for there is no bread, neither is there any water; and our soul loatheth this light bread."* *(Numbers 11:4, 21:5)*

"Our soul hates this bread…" God forbid! Jesus is the Manna come down from heaven!

> *"This is that bread which came down from heaven: not as your fathers did eat manna, and are dead: he that eateth of this bread shall live for ever."* *(John 6:58)*

What they were really saying was how Jesus wasn't enough for them!
The account of the Israelites in the desert is a reflection of what occurs in our minds today. We see how the children of Israel responded, and we think:
"How could they do that? Didn't they see what God did for them in Egypt? I would never say that if I were in their position!"
However unlikely, it's possible we wouldn't have… nevertheless, we do this in our minds all the time! We're quick to judge the children of Israel's behavior, but we're not far from following in their footsteps at times.

Like the Israelites' deliverance from Pharaoh, we also experienced God's deliverance from the devil… but we question if He will defeat the "giants" in our minds. We sing songs about our salvation, like the children of Israel did upon exiting Egypt… yet we tirelessly consider going back when things get difficult. We get a little thirsty, a little hungry, and right away, our souls despise the manna and cry out for what we were used to.

Remember, all these things were written for this cause:

"Now these things were our examples, to the intent we should not lust after evil things, as they also lusted." (1ˢᵗ Corinthians 10:6)

Unquestionably, this was written for our benefit. Proceeding in the book of Corinthians, Paul clearly relates the children of Israel to us:

"Neither be ye idolaters, as were some of them; as it is written, The people sat down to eat and drink, and rose up to play. Neither let us commit fornication, as some of them committed, and fell in one day three and twenty thousand. Neither let us tempt Christ, as some of them also tempted, and were destroyed of serpents. Neither murmur ye, as some of them also murmured, and were destroyed of the destroyer. Now all these things happened unto them for ensamples: and they are written for our admonition, upon whom the ends of the world are come." (1ˢᵗ Corinthians 10:7-11)

Idolatry is looking unto something more than the Lord. We may not have danced unclothed around a golden calf, but we forge idols in the private areas of our minds all the same. Nothing is hidden from the Lord!

We must remember what He delivered us from, and not entertain the possibility of going back. We must learn from the children of Israel's example so not to fall after the same manner. In order not to look back, we must trust Him in what's ahead. The manna He's prepared will surely prepare us.

Passion Without Preparation

We touched briefly on manna in chapter three: *Out of Egypt*. We spoke about the kneading troughs and how it was the instrument they used to make bread when in Egypt. It's all they were used to; it's all they knew. They were there for over 400 years!

At the time of the Exodus, the Israelites had learned their ways from their parents, who in turn had learned their ways from their parents, who learned it from theirs… and so on. They were submerged in the ways of Egypt. What wisdom for God to not have taken them directly into the promised land; they were nowhere near ready!

A child will say with such confidence: *"I can do it… I know how to do it!"*

"Also, that the soul be without knowledge, it is not good; and he that hasteth with his feet sinneth." (Proverbs 19:2)

"For I bear them record that they have a zeal of God, but not according to knowledge." (Romans 10:2)

If we have zeal without knowledge, we can do more harm than good. We may be confident that "we can do it," yet we lack the knowledge and experience only gained through time.

We may find ourselves like Ahimaaz, the man who outran Cushi to report to King David. Through zeal alone, he was quick to tell the king nothing of importance, and was told to turn aside:

"Then said Ahimaaz the son of Zadok yet again to Joab, But howsoever, let me, I pray thee, also run after Cushi. And Joab said, Wherefore wilt thou run, my son, seeing that thou hast no tidings ready? But howsoever, said he, let me run. And he said unto him, Run. Then Ahimaaz ran by the way of the plain, and overran Cushi…And the king said, Is the young man Absalom safe? And Ahimaaz answered, When Joab sent the king's servant, and me thy servant, I saw a great tumult, but I knew not what it was. And the king said unto him, Turn aside, and stand here. And he turned aside, and stood still." (2nd Samuel 18:22-23, 29-30)

Our confidence does not come from zeal itself, but from the knowledge of Jesus Christ. If these two men are a similitude of our conscience at times, it's best to wait. One part of us may want to outrun the other in immaturity, but the other part will arrive later with the full picture. It is not presumption or haste that will cause our inheritance, but faith and patience.

Trusting the manna God has prepared for us at His table will enable us to grow in health and maturity.

Our soul, like a child, may scream out for dessert before dinner. It may cry out for self-indulgence and may demand attention, but our parents know best. God knows how to satisfy us, which doesn't involve the spoiling of our dinner through lust and haste. When our soul cries out in hunger, we cannot afford to react as Esau, who hastily sold his birthright to Jacob for stew. Our souls will say: *"We are at the point to die, give us something to eat!"*

This is obviously not true. Esau despised his emotional decision and never regained what he gave away. We may not lose our birthright, but when we give in to our emotions in the heat of the moment, we walk away saying: *"I knew better."*

Certainly, you did! Your conscience was telling you to wait, but your unbridled soul needed it now.

Isn't it interesting that Jacob was wiser, yet Esau was hasty and emotional?

"And the LORD said unto her, Two nations are in thy womb, and two manner of people shall be separated from thy bowels; and the one people shall be stronger than the other people; and the elder shall serve the younger." (Genesis 25:23)

We need to get a foothold on our soul, like Jacob did to Esau upon his birth.

When we become born-again, the "older" soul must now serve the "younger" spirit. Our soul once made up all that we were, and now it must make way for the baby brother. The newborn spirit now gets all the attention, and our soul naturally begins to act out! However, we can't give in to a crying soul:

"Chasten thy son while there is hope, and let not thy soul spare for his crying." (Proverbs 19:18)

Like a child, our soul will always think it knows best. For this cause, we must allow the manna to wean us:

"Surely I have behaved and quieted myself, as a child that is weaned of his mother: my soul is even as a weaned child." (Psalm 131:2)

"When I was a child, I spake as a child, I understood as a child, I thought as a child: but when I became a man, I put away childish things." (1st Corinthians 13:11)

God's word will prune, purge, and purify us. It will wean us from the world and its ways, and altogether transform us. We must rely on the manna from heaven to change our tastes and desires! We need to be childlike in our approach to God and His ways, but not childlike in behavior.

"Foolishness is bound in the heart of a child; but the rod of correction shall drive it far from him." (Proverbs 22:15)

There is foolishness bound within our soul that only God's word can drive away. God's word is the rod that will spank our soul into maturity.

Mindful

"I had fainted, unless I had believed to see the goodness of the LORD in the land of the living." (Psalm 27:13)

I recall attending Bible school and having to trust God with His manna. I had to forsake all remembrance of the bread and leeks of Egypt.

When we step into the unfamiliar, our minds try to regain control of the way things were. We begin to magnify the past and long for the familiar. Consequently, we quench our hope and faith in the process.

When we allow our minds to wander, or entertain any possibility of returning to where we came from, we open the door for the enemy to take us out in unbelief. It is important to submit our minds to the process and allow them to be weaned of familiarity. We're tempted when we begin to go back to where we came from in our hearts.

"And truly, if they had been mindful of that country from whence they came out, they might have had opportunity to have returned." (Hebrews 11:15)

The important word in this passage is *mindful*. It is one thing to have fleeting thoughts, or undergo temptation, but another thing altogether when our minds are *full* of consideration of where we came from. If we go home long enough in our minds, our actions will follow.

During my enrollment at college, I worked in the security department. Each school year, we were given the names and pictures of new students to familiarize ourselves with. As the months progressed, so did the number of students who withdrew.

I remember seeing line after line of student's names struck through with a marker:

"Withdrawn... withdrawn... dismissed... withdrawn... dismissed."

It was truly disappointing to know there was such joy, expectation, and potential in each student who withdrew. Some were close friends! I often thought to myself, *"what changed?"* How can someone be *so* sure they heard from God to come to school, only to be sure to leave?

I would often counsel those who considered leaving in hopes to remind them:

"God hasn't changed His mind due to the circumstances you're facing, so why have you? Just hold on, this will pass! You're facing resistance, this is normal... but don't let this circumstance drown out the voice of God; let God's voice be heard above it."

Some would hear, some had made up their minds regardless. Unfortunately, they allowed difficulty to cloud their perspective. They no longer saw clearly.

I remember the cloudy mountain roads of Colorado. Sometimes, it would get so foggy that we'd have to pull over and wait before continuing. Otherwise, an accident was inevitable. Now, the road hadn't changed, only the weather had. The weather comes and goes, but the road remains the same. Like our walk with God, if fog were to roll over our path and cloud our view, we need to pull over and rest.

Becoming still before God in confusion is what the enemy hates! He wants us acting out emotionally. A hasty decision may leave us with only regret. Be aware. The devil sent the fog in hopes of making you question the path. He wants you confounded and afraid. He wants you to focus on the fog! He wants to have you turn around and go back! Plant your feet on God's sure path and disregard the momentary fog. This too shall pass.

In light of this, the Lord showed me the importance of relying on our training.

I studied martial arts along with my cousin John for most of my life. We trained through kata and grappling for many years, in hopes of becoming proficient in self-defense. Many thousands of single blocks, double blocks, kicks, and punches later, we rely on blocking most strikes without having to think about it. We rely on our training. Likewise, believers need to rely on their training as well.

A believer's training should cause a reaction, unlike anything else. That reaction is becoming *still*.

Rest is the reaction to the cares of life. Through many thousands of references to scripture and countless hours of meditation on God's word: we become still in the chaos. This is our defense! An effective "martial artist" of the faith should always react in peace to a stressful situation. Anxiety is simply a fruit of not believing God. It will prove we have not trusted Him at His word. Rest will always prove we have.

Rest is tied to not looking back. You'll stay calm, and look unto Jesus, rather than the circumstance, and retreat. The enemy wants you to step back and fall; the Lord wants you to stand strong and advance from a position of rest.

During my enrollment, the temptation to give in may have been present, but I wasn't *mindful* of it. Sure, the thought came often, but I couldn't afford to conceive and give it birth. When you take the option of quitting off the table, you can make an uncompromising decision when faced with adversity.

Hold On

> *"And these are they likewise which are sown on stony ground; who, when they have heard the word, immediately receive it with gladness; And have no root in themselves, and so endure but for a time: afterward, when affliction or persecution ariseth for the word's sake, immediately they are offended." (Mark 4:16, 17)*

See, we're not persecuted for *our* sake. We're persecuted for the *word's* sake. Our defense is holding on to God's word in rest because the word in our hearts is what the enemy is after.

If the devil can waste us in the wilderness, he can interrupt everyone else we're destined to touch. If the enemy succeeded in ruling Jesus out in the wilderness, we would have been altogether hopeless; thorns and thistles would've compassed the Rose of Sharon, and hell would've been our eternal life.

Consider if the one who ministered salvation to you was sidetracked! Thank God for their compassion and obedience! Imagine if Abraham didn't believe. If David was taken out by Goliath. If Moses drowned in the river. If *you* hadn't held on to the faith once delivered. If you had turned back!

You have a destiny, and it involves bringing freedom to a lost world around you. Therefore stand, and having done all else… stand!

It is the *good* fight of faith because He has already won the battle! We are called to stand fast in His armor, contending for the faith He delivered unto us. We contend by disregarding everything in contradiction to what our Father said. We contend by fixing our eyes on Jesus. We contend by believing God.

The enemy hates us getting a revelation of Jesus because an encounter with Him will transform us. The devil doesn't necessarily care about your weekly attendance of church. He won't care if you say a ritualistic prayer each night before bed. However, I assure you, he cares if you start reading God's word and believing it. He isn't frightened of a religious convert, but he is terrified of a true believer.

I have heard it said from the liberal left in how they don't care if we "go to church," they only care if we read the Bible and believe it. They must have slipped in revealing their fears. The enemy knows the danger of God's word rooted in the hearts of true believers because it is the increasing demise of his kingdom on earth. So, he will do whatever he can to keep the church at bay.

"Be sober, be vigilant; because your adversary the devil, as a roaring lion, walketh about, seeking whom he may devour." (1st Peter 5:8)

This passage is referring to the sobriety of our minds. The battleground is in our soul. The war was won in our spirit, but the battle for our mind is daily waged. Therefore, be mindful of Him rather than where you came from. We give over the ground in our minds when we look back to Egypt, rather than looking back at the cross. You decide what to be mindful of.

Stand fast, take courage, and only believe. Only believe what God's word says. You have the potential to change the lives of countless people. Don't succumb to the enemy's fear tactics, he's already been overcome by Jesus. Like the giants on borrowed time, so is the devil afraid of you!

Cup Of Offense

To revisit Mark, chapter 4, the enemy tries to bait us with an offense. This will hook, line, and sink us if swallowed. I've seen this all too often. I have also come to notice how, in general, the body of Christ has become too easily offended. The truth is, we don't have the right to be offended in the first place.

"Great peace have they which love thy law: and nothing shall offend them." (Psalm 119:165)

This verse speaks volumes. See, if you cherish and esteem God's word above all, you won't consider any *other* word. You'll be left with peace instead of bitterness and envy. If you were only to accept the word of God, you'd never settle for the words of man. When we allow other words to have more weight in our hearts than God's, we set ourselves up for failure.

Offense is often *taken* due to unfulfilled expectations. We may have placed an expectation upon someone, and they didn't meet that expectation, and we could have taken offense. We may have expected an outcome that came nowhere near what we imagined, and afterward, taken offense. When we place expectations in a person or a circumstance, discontentment is surely to follow.

"I really expected them to do that...Well, I didn't expect that..." (Even the statement, *"that was better than I expected,"* could be proven insecure. For if the situation proved worse than expected, you could've easily been disappointed! Our expectation should be in God alone.)

Offense is often wrapped in a package with justification as the ribbon in which we pull to open it. It's a deceitful gift from the enemy delivered to our doorstep. We begin to unwrap it by justifying the offense in our minds:

"You know if they were only thinking about someone other than themselves for a change... I can't believe they said that to me! I can't believe this happened... I didn't deserve this."

"What is this?"

The truth is, the justification we deserved was death. As I recall, while Jesus was dying on the cross for those who placed Him there, He cried out: "Father forgive them, they don't know what they're doing" (Luke 23:34). If anyone had the right to justify themselves, it was Jesus; yet He opened not His mouth.

Offense is the poison and bait of the devil. The instant it touches our tongue, we must spit it out. Otherwise, we'll have a hook in our mouths. We need to train our senses to discern the danger of offense, and completely cut it off. Our souls need to be transformed and weaned from the ways of the world.

Honey

When you cut out processed sugar for over a month, your taste buds will change. You'll begin to lose weight, experience more energy, and altogether feel great! Leading up to that month however, you'll go through significant withdrawal, but afterward, you'll have a different palate.

After some time, if you happen to eat the sugary foods you were used to, you'll find it inedible. You'll wonder how you even lived like that for that long! You cut out the substitute sugar that your mouth had grown accustomed to. God wants to replace that sugar with honey. His word is so much sweeter.

> *"How sweet are thy words unto my taste! yea, sweeter than honey to my mouth!" (Psalm 119:103)*

It may become bitter in the belly because of the process, but afterward, the taste buds of your soul will change. When a contradictory thought even touches your soul, you'll quickly spit it out because it doesn't taste the same. God's word is the sugar we need for our energy source.

Have you ever had a sweet and juicy fruit, and wondered:

"Why haven't I been eating fruit like this all along?"

Why do we replace vegetables with sugary drinks and snacks? Why do we allow our souls to have substituted nutrition? Fruits and honey are not only sweeter but undeniably better. We must have this same approach towards the nourishment of our soul. We can't afford to read a few passages of God's pure honey, and then allow the substitute sugar of this world to fill the rest of the glass. God's word is all we need. The more we eat, the more we want. The honey of His manna changes our desires.

Open Door Policy

Regarding offense, there is wisdom I've learned when ministering unto others. I leave my heart open and vulnerable to those I'm serving, insomuch that it's possible to be hurt. In ministry, you'll always be faced with the opportunity to take offense, just be wise and don't!

If you were to slowly close your heart towards those who you are serving due to fear of getting hurt, you would be robbing them of your full potential, and you would be robbing yourself of theirs. If you are serving someone with less than all your heart, you are operating out of fear and not love.

For example: if you were trying to disciple the tenth believer that the Lord had placed in your life, but the other nine had hurt you, you would have closed yourself off little by little from each brother or sister along the way. Each believer in progression would have been ministered to in more and more fear. Fear of being hurt, fear of being rejected.

Now, if you had ministered to the nine, and all had wronged you, but you suffered loss and cast your care upon the Lord; If you had considered yourself dead, hidden in Christ, and had given up the right to be offended when you were baptized; If you had forgiven them as Christ had freely forgiven you: then, you could have effectively ministered to this precious brother or sister in the Lord. You could have ministered with a heart full of love, regardless of what the others had said or done.

However, if you were closed off in fear of becoming hurt again, you would never have effectively ministered to those who truly needed it. These brothers and sisters could have drawn from the Christ in you! They needed what you had to offer, but because of fear, you never gave them a chance. You would have allowed condition to dictate the unconditional love of God.

We must allow our hearts to be soft towards God and His people. We cannot afford to harden our hearts and allow them to become impenetrable due to our pasts. If our hearts are hardened, it's because we've allowed what others to have said, become more important than what God did. To be un-offendable, we must esteem what He says above everything else.

"Also take no heed unto all words that are spoken; lest thou hear thy servant curse thee: For oftentimes also thine own heart knoweth that thou thyself likewise hast cursed others." (Ecclesiastes 7:21, 22)

What Solomon is saying here is that we should be careful not to take into consideration everything that's spoken, whether good or bad. Beware of constant criticism and praise. Both could take you out. We should only take God's word to heart.

Tagging off the same verse, we should also consider when hearing others speak negatively towards us, that we have also done it to others. We need to walk around with a heart full of forgiveness rather than a heart easily offended. We must be ready to forgive our brother before the offense even takes place! He who seeks to forgive and disregard an offense is one who seeks love.

Words are heavy, especially the words from friends and family. The enemy knows this, so we ought to be aware of his strategy beforehand. He will try his best to use those closest to you to cause offense:

"Yea, mine own familiar friend, in whom I trusted, which did eat of my bread, hath lifted up his heel against me...For it was not an enemy that reproached me; then I could have borne it: neither was it he that hated me that did magnify himself against me; then I would have hid myself from him: But it was thou, a man mine equal, my guide, and mine acquaintance. We took sweet counsel together, and walked unto the house of God in company." (Psalm 41:9, 55:12-14)

It's always going to be those who are closest to you that have the most potential to offend you. Their words will have the most impact. So, we must have more expectation in the Lord than we do anyone else! If our best friend was to turn on us, or our mother or father were to curse us, we must have what God says about us hold the most weight. God's word should have enough impact alone, that all other words fall to the back of the line. They should fall off a cliff into the sea of forgetfulness.

It is inevitable that people will offend, but it is foolish for us to take it. When the temptation of offense comes knocking at the door of our heart, we cannot even afford to say, *"who is it?"*

Now, it is appropriate, and necessary even, to allow those who are close to you to have counsel in your life. Bearing in mind, they are not your affirmation, your confidence, or your counselor: God alone is. What God's word says about you alone is all that matters.

Crying Out For Quail

"And he gave them their request; but sent leanness into their soul." (Psalm 106:15)

Did you know that someone can starve to death by overeating rabbit? Eating it alone could lead to malnutrition and "rabbit starvation" because of the leanness of the meat.

In the book of Numbers, the Lord sent quail to the people upon their request. It was given in mounds around three feet high, which covered the whole face of the ground. It was more than they could've ever wanted! The people lusted over it and gathered as much as they could handle. This displeased the Lord, and while the quail was yet in their mouth, He sent forth a plague (Numbers 11:33).

This is a tremendous lesson for us. Lusting after the flesh will only cause leanness to our souls; it can never satisfy. The more you have, the more you'll want. It leads to malnutrition and starvation, and it ultimately profits nothing.

Have you ever found yourself scrolling on news feeds via social media or watching video, after video on your phone, only to be left drained and unsatisfied in the end? Feeding the flesh is a bottomless pit that will only lead to your starvation. It will never satisfy. The more quail you cry out for and indulge, the more you find yourself wanting.

Consider the awesome description of Manna:

"And when the dew that lay was gone up, behold, upon the face of the wilderness there lay a small round thing, as small as the hoar frost on the ground...And the house of Israel called the name thereof Manna: and it was like coriander seed, white; and the taste of it was like wafers made with honey." (Exodus 16:14, 31)

This small white substance would be all that they would need to live in the desert. It would arrive upon the dew each morning and would satisfy every mouth in Israel. Not as the heaps of quail which brought leanness, but a small white seed that brought fulfillment. I especially love the way they would prepare it:

"And the people went about, and gathered it, and ground it in mills, or beat it in a mortar, and baked it in pans, and made cakes of it: and the taste of it was as the taste of fresh oil." (Numbers 11:8)

This is a depiction of us meditating on His word! We need to rise and gather the word, mixing it with faith by grinding it in our hearts!

"This book of the law shall not depart out of thy mouth, but thou shalt meditate therein day and night..." (Joshua 1:8)

Our soul may cry out for quail, but we need to muse on the Manna. When the small honey wafer becomes the biggest thing of all, you'll find yourself lying down in green pastures; perfect, entire, and wanting nothing. Truly, Jesus alone is our satisfaction.

Chapter Seven

The Ark

From the pattern shown to Moses on the mountain to the building of the Tabernacle; From the priests and their garments to the artificers and the instruments forged; From the building of the Ark to its carrying into the temple: this all spoke of One work, unconceived nor built by man, but God: The Ark of our New Covenant, Jesus Christ.

In this chapter, we will speak of God's glory found in the Ark of the Covenant. Afterward, we will journey with Joshua right into the promised land.

This Holy God

"What are we going to do with this Ark?"

The Philistines were seven months into their affliction by the hand of God and they finally seemed to have enough. *Seven months... really?* The Lord was destroying the city and the people, and the ones who didn't die were struck with tumors and hemorrhoids.

"How shall we send it back to Israel?" They asked.

The priests and the diviners were then summoned for consultation. They had to make an entreaty, and send the Ark back favorably, so not to cause a greater offense.

Their counsel was to make figures of what was troubling them and place them within the Ark (five golden tumors, and five golden mice, according to the number of the Philistine lords). Afterward, they placed it on a new cart with two "milking" cows that had never been yoked before. This was sent as a trespass offering so that they might be healed.

This account parallels Moses forging the brazen serpent and fastening it to the pole: whoever looked upon the cause of their harm was healed. The Philistines were foolish to have held the Ark for that long, but the priests were wise to entreat the Lord in this manner.

The Philistine's plan was this: if the cows cooperated and went straight towards the Israelites, they would know the Lord brought all this evil upon them. However, if the cows went another way, then it was all by chance. A slim chance, nonetheless. This plan would truly prove if the God of the Ark of the Covenant was behind this or not.

Firstly, you cannot yoke two cows together that haven't been yoked to an older, more experienced one initially. The two will not agree with each other, and will certainly not walk peacefully. Even if you were to join the unyoked cow, with an older, more experienced one, the younger would not go without a fight.

The Bible says:

"The kine took the straight way to the way of Beth-shemesh, and went along the highway, lowing as they went, and turned not aside to the right hand or to the left..." (1st Samuel 6:12)

They were Philistine cows that went peacefully in a way they had never gone before. They weren't even Israeli cows!

Secondly, you'd want to use oxen, not milk cows. It's common to castrate an ox to use for plowing so that he is easier to control.

Thirdly, the Philistines used two dairy cows whose calves were just born. These cows would have never left their newborns at home! So, not only did these Philistine dairy cows leave their calves behind without consideration... they went peacefully down an unfamiliar road without ever having been yoked before. This was altogether miraculous!

They soon made their way into the field of Joshua, where the people were reaping their wheat harvest. Upon the Ark's entrance, the people lifted their eyes and rejoiced! They broke up the wood from the cart and sacrificed these cows unto the Lord. Afterward, they carried the Ark back into the city.

Jesus' glory is evident in this passage.

Remember when Jesus was on the Mount of Olives (where He ascended, and where He will soon return) and told the two disciples to bring Him an ass and a colt?

...Go into the village over against you, and straightway ye shall find an ass tied, and a colt with her: loose them, and bring them unto me." (Matthew 21:2)

"Rejoice greatly, O daughter of Zion; shout, O daughter of Jerusalem: behold, thy King cometh unto thee: he is just, and having salvation; lowly, and riding upon an ass, and upon a colt the foal of an ass." (Zechariah 9:9)

In the book of Mark, it says: "*Where no man sat before.*" These animals were never ridden! Jesus then made His way through Jerusalem the week before Passover. The people rejoiced to see Him, and cried: "*Hosanna in the highest,*" which upon interpretation means: save, help from on high!

Jesus was the wheat harvest that the Bethshemites were reaping! They lifted their eyes and rejoiced to see the Ark, like the people cried Hosanna upon Jesus' entrance.

It's of no coincidence that the Ark was brought into the field of Joshua (another name for Yeshua, or, Jesus) to the great stone of Abel. In other words: the field of Jesus.

We are Jesus' field!

"...even unto the great stone of Abel, whereon they set down the ark of the LORD: which stone remaineth unto this day in the field of Joshua, the Bethshemite" (1ˢᵗ Samuel 6:18)

Jesus said if the people which cried Hosanna had held their peace, the stones would have immediately cried out. I believe He was referring to this occurrence.

He poured out his blood for us like the cows were sacrificed. He was the Ark of the Covenant that rode upon the back of the unyoked animals. He ushered in the presence of God for all mankind by peacefully surrendering to death.

"...he is brought as a lamb to the slaughter, and as a sheep before her shearers is dumb, so he openeth not his mouth." (Isaiah 53:7)

He carried the cross up the mountain and was slain on Golgotha's hill. His was the true Righteous Blood, of the "righteous blood" of Abel and Zechariah that were slain (Matt. 23:35). As Abel was murdered, so was Jesus. His blood satisfied the cry of Hosanna, and the blood of Abel crying out from the ground.

Furthermore, the priests bearing the Ark across Jordan correlate greatly with this occurrence:

*"And they commanded the people, saying, When ye see the ark of the covenant of the LORD your God, and the priests the Levites bearing it, then ye shall remove from your place, and go after it. Yet there shall be a space between you and it, about two thousand cubits by measure: come not near unto it, that ye may know the way by which ye must go: **for ye have not passed this way heretofore.**" (Joshua 3:3, 4) (emphasis mine)*

Like the cows were unfamiliar with the journey ahead, so were the children of Israel with theirs. Consider what happened when the priests stepped foot in the Jordan:

"And as they that bare the ark were come unto Jordan, and the feet of the priests that bare the ark were dipped in the brim of the water, (for Jordan overfloweth all his banks all the time of harvest,) That the waters which came down from above stood and rose up upon an heap very far from the city Adam, that is beside Zaretan: and those that came down toward the sea of the plain, even the salt sea, failed, and were cut off: and the people passed over right against Jericho." (Joshua 3:15, 16)

The waters of sin that flowed from Adam were cut off by the Last Adam completely.

The passage also mentions how Jordan overflows its banks in harvest. Like the cows bearing the Ark came to the field of Joshua during harvest, so did the priests dip their feet in Jordan's harvest. This whole account speaks of the Christ to come. Jesus is our harvest; He was sown in death so we could reap His life.

"Verily, verily, I say unto you, Except a corn of wheat fall into the ground and die, it abideth alone: but if it die, it bringeth forth much fruit." (John 12:24)

One last thought. Like us, these cows left a foreign land to enter the new Jerusalem. They left their family, their masters, and their idols behind. They found themselves yoked to a new Master, journeying on a path they had never travelled before. They became witnesses and sacrificed their lives for the Lord.

Let us also sacrifice the life we once lived by yoking ourselves unto Jesus, journeying with the Presence of God, carrying within us the milk of God's word, and causing the hopeless to lift their eyes and cry, Hosanna!

The Rebellion Of Korah

"Aarons rod that Budded"

"And after the second veil, the tabernacle which is called the Holiest of all; Which had the golden censer, and the ark of the covenant overlaid round about with gold, wherein was the golden pot that had manna, and Aaron's rod that budded, and the tables of the covenant." (Hebrews 9:3, 4)

The rebellion of Korah is an extraordinary account worth examining together to reveal Christ within.

There are three major points to be addressed.

1. The rebellion of Korah and the relation to the devil.

2. The rebellion and its relation to man.

3. The rebellion and it's relation to Jesus.

First, let's discuss the account itself, and afterward elaborate.

"Now Korah, the son of Izhar, the son of Kohath, the son of Levi, and Dathan and Abiram, the sons of Eliab, and On, the son of Peleth, sons of Reuben, took men: And they rose up before Moses, with certain of the children of Israel, two hundred and fifty princes of the assembly, famous in the congregation, men of renown: And they gathered themselves together against Moses and against Aaron, and said unto them, Ye take too much upon you, seeing all the congregation are holy, every one of them, and the LORD is among them: wherefore then lift ye up yourselves above the congregation of the LORD? And when Moses heard it, he fell upon his face." (Numbers 16:1-4)

Convinced they should have preeminence in the camp, Korah, Dathan and Abiram revolted against Moses and Aaron. They had their eyes on their mantle's altogether.

Moses then rebuked Korah, and called upon Dathan and Abiram to show themselves. They said Egypt was the land flowing with milk and honey they were delivered from, and how they were brought by Moses' pride into the wilderness to die.

Wow… they just called Egypt the promised land.

The utter rebellion and pride!

"...for out of the abundance of the heart the mouth speaketh." (Matthew 12:34)

Truly, there was only wickedness in their hearts. These were the men that saw themselves fit to lead the congregation? No, these men weren't interested in serving... in their prideful pursuit of the throne, they were only looking to be exalted.

Korah, his company, and Aaron, were then told to bring censors of fire and incense before the Lord. Afterward, Korah stood before the door of the Tabernacle and gathered the whole congregation against Moses. He was forming a rebellion and looking to takeover!

Consequently, the Lord commanded Moses, Aaron, and the congregation to separate themselves from Korah and his company. Moses proved his works were ordained of God by asking for the earth to swallow the rebellious alive, which happened instantaneously. Shortly after, a fire from the Lord consumed the 250 princes who burnt incense.

The whole congregation then brought slander upon Moses and Aaron the following day by saying they "killed the people of the Lord." *Can you believe it?*

"There is no fear of God before their eyes." (Romans 3:18)

In conclusion, a plague broke out and consumed 14,700 of the congregants, while Aaron stood with an atonement between the dead and the living.

Original Pride

Rebellion of Satan against God
First to discuss will be the rebellion of Korah following suit after his father, the devil. This account correlates well to Satan's original pride. His eyes were fixed on the throne and was ungrateful for all that God had given him. The following passages should speak for themselves:

"Thou art the anointed cherub that covereth; and I have set thee so...Thou wast perfect in thy ways from the day that thou wast created, till iniquity was found in thee...therefore I will cast thee as profane out of the mountain of God: and I will destroy thee...Thine heart was lifted up because of thy beauty, thou hast corrupted thy wisdom by reason of thy brightness: I will cast thee to the ground...therefore will I bring forth a fire from the midst of thee, it shall devour thee, and I will bring thee to ashes upon the earth in the sight of all them that behold thee." (Ezekiel 28:14-18)

"Ye are of your father the devil, and the lusts of your father ye will do..." (John 8:44)

"And Korah gathered all the congregation against them unto the door of the tabernacle of the congregation: and the glory of the LORD appeared unto all the congregation. And the LORD spake unto Moses and unto Aaron, saying, Separate yourselves from among this congregation, that I may consume them in a moment." (Numbers 16:19-21)

See, Korah and his company were just following in their father's footsteps.

"And Moses said unto Korah, Hear, I pray you, ye sons of Levi: Seemeth it but a small thing unto you, that the God of Israel hath separated you from the congregation of Israel, to bring you near to himself to do the service of the tabernacle of the LORD, and to stand before the congregation to minister unto them? And he hath brought thee near to him, and all thy brethren the sons of Levi with thee: and seek ye the priesthood also?" (Numbers 16:8-10)

Everything performed before Christ was a foreshadow of the One to come. Seeking the Priesthood, in this case, was as seeking the position only held by Jesus. For the devil, it wasn't enough to have been in the position he was in, he wanted to be like God.

"How art thou fallen from heaven, O Lucifer, son of the morning! how art thou cut down to the ground, which didst weaken the nations! For thou hast said in thine heart, I will ascend into heaven, I will exalt my throne above the stars of God: I will sit also upon the mount of the congregation, in the sides of the north: I will ascend above the heights of the clouds; I will be like the most High. Yet thou shalt be brought down to hell, to the sides of the pit." (Isaiah 14:12-15)

The devil had his eyes set on Jesus' position, as Korah had his eyes set on Moses'. God set Lucifer in the position he was in... but it wasn't enough.

The earth having swallowed up the company of Korah, led me to consider the fate of the beast and false prophet:

"And I saw the beast, and the kings of the earth, and their armies, gathered together to make war against him that sat on the horse, and against his army. And the beast was taken, and with him the false prophet that wrought miracles before him, with which he deceived them that had received the mark of the beast, and them that worshipped his image. These both were cast alive into a lake of fire burning with brimstone. And the remnant were slain with the sword of him that sat upon the horse, which sword proceeded out of his mouth: and all the fowls were filled with their flesh." (Revelation 19:19-21)

A similar fate for a similar rebellion. Korah's company was swallowed alive by the earth, and the 250 princes succeeded in death by fire. Similarly, the beast and false prophet will be swallowed alive by a pit of fire beneath the earth, with all the remnants to follow in death.

The Rebellion Of Man

There is a great correlation between the previous accounts, but it is important to consider the event itself: Korah, the *man,* rebelled against Moses.

Man was caught in the middle of this one. Not to say, by any means, that man was innocent; on the contrary, man was held accountable for sin entering the world. The cost of our disobedience was the greatest price to have paid: we were cast out of the presence of the Lord.

On that day, we lost paradise; We lost our innocent consciences and saw ourselves naked; We lost our dominion and authority; We were separated from God, and most regrettably, we lost our right-standing with Him. The cost of our transgression was death; the estimated worth of what we lost was incalculable.

Thankfully, the fate of man's rebellion is unlike that of the devil. When it came to Lucifer's rebellion: he was cast out of heaven without redemption. On the other hand, when it came to man's rebellion: Jesus was the Lamb slain before the foundation of the world.

The Lord had Calvary in mind before we ever rebelled. He knew that giving us His breath would one day cost Him His. Yet He made us still.

"And the LORD God formed man of the dust of the ground, and breathed into his nostrils the breath of life; and man became a living soul." (Genesis 2:7)

The difference between us, the animals, and the angels, is the most important of all: we were created in His own image and likeness! We were very good in His sight!

"And God said, Let us make man in our image, after our likeness..." (Genesis 1:26)

Now, what I meant by man being caught in the middle was how the devil used us against God. We were responsible for our rebellious decision, but the enemy was the instigator. For this cause, the snake was cursed above all the animals.

"And the LORD God said unto the woman, What is this that thou hast done? And the woman said, The serpent beguiled me, and I did eat. And the LORD God said unto the serpent, Because thou hast done this, thou art cursed...And unto Adam he said, Because thou hast hearkened unto the voice of thy wife, and hast eaten of the tree, of which I commanded thee, saying, Thou shalt not eat of it: cursed is the ground for thy sake; in sorrow shalt thou eat of it all the days of thy life." (Genesis 3:13-14, 17)

Notice how the ground was cursed for man's sake, but not man himself. Yet the snake itself was cursed. This is because man holds within himself something no other creature has: God's image and likeness.

Adam and Eve saw themselves naked after eating from the tree, and afterward sowed fig leaves together for a covering; The Lord made them coats of skins instead. This foreshadowed the sacrifice and mercy to come. Jesus would be the offering who would truly clothe man's nakedness.

The Obedience Of Jesus

The resolve of this account leaves us with a beautiful depiction of our Lord Jesus.

"And the LORD spake unto Moses, saying, Speak unto the children of Israel, and take of every one of them a rod according to the house of their fathers, of all their princes according to the house of their fathers twelve rods: write thou every man's name upon his rod...And it came to pass, that on the morrow Moses went into the tabernacle of witness; and, behold, the rod of Aaron for the house of Levi was budded, and brought forth buds, and bloomed blossoms, and yielded almonds...And the LORD said unto Moses, Bring Aaron's rod again before the testimony, to be kept for a token against the rebels; and thou shalt quite take away their murmurings from me, that they die not." (Numbers 17:1-2, 8, 10)

I was looking for Jesus as for why Aaron's rod was placed in the Ark of the Covenant. As for the golden pot which had manna, and the tablets of stone, I speculated as to the significance of Jesus… but Aaron's rod? Where was the significance? Well, researching almonds led me right to Him.

The scripture says Aaron's rod yielded almonds. When almonds bud, and the flowers on its tree blossom, it's known as the harbinger of spring. They bud at winter's end, indicating spring has come. The almond tree is also known as "the awakening tree" because it's the first tree to blossom in Israel.

Aaron's rod was a dead stick which brought forth life. The word of the Lord caused it to blossom! This foretells of Jesus' resurrection. The rod represents authority; Jesus alone would have the authority to lay His life down and raise it up again.

Jesus was sown in the dead of winter's sin; right in the middle of our rebellion. He is our first fruits! He is the indication that winter has passed.

We gave up our life when we ate from the tree of the knowledge of good and evil. Nevertheless, when we accept Christ as the authority to have died, and to have risen in our place, our disconnected rods are then engrafted into the tree of Life.

There are yet a few more things to discuss concerning Korah's rebellion. For one, Korah, (like the enemy initially did towards God, and will do again with the rebellious nations) gathered everyone against Moses and Aaron. They were left alone.

"The kings of the earth set themselves, and the rulers take counsel together, against the LORD, and against his anointed, saying." (Psalm 2:2)

Jesus was left alone with the whole assembly of the Jews against Him.

"He came unto his own, and his own received him not." (John 1:11)

They cried:

"...Crucify him, crucify him." (Luke 23:21

Jesus was going to be the Barabbas in our place. For our sedition, rebellion, murder, etc., Jesus would be the scapegoat.

Barabbas' name means: *son of the father*. Bar, meaning: *son of*; and Abba, meaning: *father*. Jesus, the true *Son of the Father*, would die for our rebellion. Barabbas represents mankind in this regard: we should have been killed, not Jesus.

Barabbas was released, Jesus was crucified.

Like Aaron's rod budded almonds in the middle of Korah's rebellion; Jesus would die and resurrect in the middle of man's rebellion.

In the true mirror of Aaron, Jesus was the atonement standing between the dead and the living that stayed the plague of sin (Numbers 16:48-50). Aaron was the high priest who offered an atonement, but Jesus was the High Priest Who *was* the atonement.

What can also be gleaned concerning Aaron is how his name means: *lofty, exalted, high mountain*. Jesus is the High and Lofty One! He would be exalted by dying upon the mountaintop for us. Korah had his eye set on the lofty position of Moses and Aaron, but that position is only held by One; our great High Priest, Jesus.

The Man, The Cross, And The Ark

The ark of Noah, the ark which held Moses, and the Ark of the Covenant all held something in common. They all carried something within... *a new beginning*.

All three painted a picture of the Ark who would walk on two feet, Jesus. He would be the Ark that stood out from all the rest… if they could look past the acacia tree.

"And they shall make an ark of shittim wood: two cubits and a half shall be the length thereof, and a cubit and a half the breadth thereof, and a cubit and a half the height thereof. And thou shalt overlay it with pure gold, within and without shalt thou overlay it, and shalt make upon it a crown of gold round about." (Exodus 25:10-11)

The wood used to build the frame of the Ark was acacia. This type of tree is found common in the deserts. It is not rare, nor is it the most beautiful; It is a thorny, gnarly-knotted tree, which grows best in dry ground.

This is astounding! Isn't it remarkable how the frame of His sanctuary (in which His presence dwelt) would be a common desert tree? Not the oak of Bashaan, or the cedar of Lebanon, but the acacia. On the outside, Jesus looked like all of us. Yet on the inside, the glory of His majesty resided.

"For he shall grow up before him as a tender plant, and as a root out of a dry ground: he hath no form nor comeliness; and when we shall see him, there is no beauty that we should desire him." (Isaiah 53:2)

(Naturally speaking) what separated Jesus from us was not the body in which He came (even though His flesh was sinless), but the pure gold inside. If the people could see past the common tree, they would be able to see the rarest tree of all: the tree of Life. The only one of its kind!

The acacia wood represents Jesus' humanity, and the pure gold represents His divinity. He was 100% man, and He was 100% God. He came as a man, but only those who "ate His flesh and drank His blood" could see the Christ within.

It's important to note how Jesus wasn't performing miracles as a young boy, or walking in the miraculous as a teenager. It was only during the wedding in Cana that His miracle ministry began:

*"This **beginning of miracles** did Jesus in Cana of Galilee, and manifested forth his glory; and his disciples believed on him." (John 2:11) (emphasis mine)*

This is precisely why the people in His hometown said:

Chapter Seven: The Ark

"Is not this the carpenter's son? is not his mother called Mary? and his brethren, James, and Joses, and Simon, and Judas?" (Matthew 13:55)

Nevertheless, Jesus truly is the Carpenter's Son: The Father's great work.

Up until that point, they were only familiar with Jesus the man, but not Jesus the Christ. Though he was subject to His parents, and known in the town as Joseph's son, He held within Himself the glory of the Father.

Jesus wasn't walking around as an extravagant king with great pomp and grandeur. It wasn't the decking of a golden crown or the allurement of kingly garments: It was the transfigured Christ upon the mountaintop within; It was the "more than Solomon" who stood before them; It was the "I AM" that existed eternally and altogether outside of time; It was the Holy of Holies beyond the veil; It was the Everlasting Father Philip asked to see.

Philip struggled for a moment to see the Father in Jesus. But Jesus responded:

"...he that hath seen me hath seen the Father..." (John 14:9)

The Father's ways were perfectly revealed in Jesus, yet veiled through His flesh at the same time.

"By a new and living way, which he hath consecrated for us, through the veil, that is to say, his flesh." (Hebrews 10:20)

Jesus was the Ark which held the new beginning for all mankind within. His flesh: the veil that was torn; His blood: the atonement for our souls.

The First-Ripe Grapes

"...Now the time was the time of the firstripe grapes." (Numbers 13:20)

"And they came unto the brook of Eshcol, and cut down from thence a branch with one cluster of grapes, and they bare it between two upon a staff; and they brought of the pomegranates, and of the figs." (Numbers 13:23)

This account has a few portrayals of Christ worth mentioning. For one, the scripture says they "bare it between two upon a staff." What was borne between these two men? The first fruits of the land of Canaan: Jesus! He died between two men at Calvary, so that He could rise again as *our* first fruits.

137

"But now is Christ risen from the dead, and become the firstfruits of them that slept. But every man in his own order: Christ the firstfruits; afterward they that are Christ's at his coming." (1st Corinthians 15:20, 23)

Another similitude is the manner the priests carried the Ark of the Covenant. They bore the Ark atop their shoulders with golden acacia staffs.

The Ark was in the center of men, wood, and gold.

Man was forbidden to touch the Ark. So, the golden wood man touched, touched the golden Ark. Signifying the concealed instrument in which God would use to allow man to enter His presence: the cross.

The cross would be the only way to touch God!

"For I determined not to know any thing among you, save Jesus Christ, and him crucified...But we speak the wisdom of God in a mystery, even the hidden wisdom, which God ordained before the world unto our glory: Which none of the princes of this world knew: for had they known it, they would not have crucified the Lord of glory." (1st Corinthians 2:2, 7-8)

They couldn't perceive it even if they wanted because It was covered. It was covered in gold! The concealment was from God. Consider Moses' staff turning into a serpent:

"And Moses answered and said, But, behold, they will not believe me, nor hearken unto my voice: for they will say, The LORD hath not appeared unto thee. And the LORD said unto him, What is that in thine hand? And he said, A rod." (Exodus 4:1-2)

The Lord answered Moses' question by pointing him to what was in his hand: the staff that defeated the serpent. We know God sent Jesus to us because of a revelation of the cross!

Moses' rod held the authority over the serpent because he picked it up by the tail. As a rule, you don't pick a snake up by the tail. You grab its' head. Typically, when you grab a snake by the head, it's because you're afraid of getting bit. But grabbing it by the tail proves you're in control.

The staff is what the Lord used to crush the serpents head, and He grabbed it by the tail to do so. The cross proved the power He held over death's sting because He resurrected.

Consider Uzzah, whose name means: *strength*. After touching the Ark bare-handed in his own strength, he was killed. He didn't come to God the right way, or rather the *only* way. The only way to touch God is through the cross of Jesus Christ.

Jesus bore the cross upon His shoulders and carried it up to Calvary. The cross was the go-between, the bridging of the gap. Jesus, the Man, bore the cross; but then at Calvary: the cross, bore Christ, the Ark. He was the great High Priest, and the offering Himself. He was the fullness of the Ark of the Covenant.

> *"Now of the things which we have spoken this is the sum: We have such an high priest, who is set on the right hand of the throne of the Majesty in the heavens; A minister of the sanctuary, and of the true tabernacle, which the Lord pitched, and not man. For every high priest is ordained to offer gifts and sacrifices: wherefore it is of necessity that this man have somewhat also to offer." (Hebrews 8:1-3)*

Bezaleel

"I have called Him by name."

Bezaleel's name means: *In the shadow of God,* or *under his protection* (Psalms 91).

> *"And the LORD spake unto Moses, saying, See, I have called by name Bezaleel the son of Uri, the son of Hur, of the tribe of Judah: And I have filled him with the spirit of God, in wisdom, and in understanding, and in knowledge, and in all manner of workmanship, To devise cunning works, to work in gold, and in silver, and in brass, And in cutting of stones, to set them, and in carving of timber, to work in all manner of workmanship. And I, behold, I have given with him Aholiab, the son of Ahisamach, of the tribe of Dan: and in the hearts of all that are wise hearted I have put wisdom, that they may make all that I have commanded thee." (Exodus 31:1-6)*

I couldn't help but notice how Bezaleel was "called by name." He was anointed by God and filled with all wisdom and understanding. He was from the tribe of Judah and was appointed as the overseeing artificer of the Tabernacle.

The Hebrew name *Uri* means: *God is my light*; and the name *Hur* means: *liberty, whiteness, hole*; The Biblical name *Judah* means: *Praise*; He was given help through *Aholiab*, whose name means: *tent of the father*; Who was the son of *Ahisamach*, whose name means: *brother, from* the tribe of *Dan*, whose name means: *he judged*. These men would oversee and construct all the holy instruments for ministry, and the Ark itself.

Through searching the meaning of these names in Hebrew, and in the order in which they are written, *(Bezaleel, Uri, Hur, Judah, Aholiab, Ahisamach, and Dan)*, I found:

Jesus was in God's shadow and under His protection; He was the Light of the world; He would fill the hole with His liberty and whiteness; He would be praised because in the tent the Father would give Him; our Brother would be judged for all mankind.

Hallelujah!

He was the *Pattern*.

> *"Who serve unto the example and shadow of heavenly things, as Moses was admonished of God when he was about to make the tabernacle: for, See, saith he, that thou make all things according to the **pattern** shewed to thee in the mount." (Hebrews 8:5) (emphasis mine)*

There were always specific instructions from God in whatever was built. Noah built the ark with specific instructions. There was specific instruction in building the Tabernacle by Moses, and the temple by Solomon. There is also specific instruction for us. The Bible is the blueprint in which we're to follow. We build with Christ as the foundation of our life. He is the Cornerstone and Rock in which we stand.

We need to follow the Pattern.

This Is My Rest Forever

The flesh of Jesus was not meant to be rooted here on earth. Jesus always wanted to root Himself in the ground of our hearts.

> *"...that they might be called trees of righteousness, the planting of the LORD, that he might be glorified." (Isaiah 61:3)*

This was always the plan!

When Moses completed the construction of the Tabernacle, and after the sacrifice was made, the glory of the Lord filled the Tabernacle, and Moses was unable to enter.

I can picture the Father thinking to Himself as a portion of His plan unfolded:

"Ok, one step closer."

Later, it is found within the heart of David to build the Lord a house. However, he is told by the prophet Nathan that the Lord would build *him* a house. His son Solomon would construct the temple instead.

After completing the temple, Solomon offered a sacrifice that couldn't be numbered. Once the minstrels were found praising the Lord in one accord, and the priests had finished placing the Ark of the Covenant in the Most Holy place, the glory of the Lord filled the temple. This left the priests unable to stand or minister!

After Solomon prayed and dedicated the temple, the fire of the Lord came down and consumed the sacrifice. Afterward, the Father possibly in His heart:

"Yes… A little closer."

After this: Jesus.

"…Behold the Lamb of God…" (John 1:29)

The Holy Spirit descended upon Jesus after baptism, filling Him without measure. He is the fullness of the Godhead bodily. The perfect manifestation of the pattern shown to Moses. The walking Ark of our new Covenant.

Jesus was then crucified in our place. He cried, *"it is finished"* upon giving up the ghost. Three days later… our resurrected Messiah! The first fruits from the dead; our righteousness!

Now, I can imagine the Father once more in His heart:

"So close…"

Now, you may think:

"So close? What do you mean?" "It's a *finished* work!"

Yes, truly it is. Hallelujah to the Lamb who was slain! It *is* finished!

Nevertheless… the disciples were told to wait. They waited and gathered in an upper room. And when the day of Pentecost arrived, and the disciples were found in one accord… *Suddenly…* A sound from heaven as a mighty rushing wind! The glory of the Lord came down in cloven tongues of fire! This time He didn't fill the Tabernacle, or the temple… through Jesus' sacrifice, He filled the people! He fills us!

No more ordinances through priests, or veils of separation, no longer mediation through men, but the Man, Christ Jesus!

Like the Tabernacle and temple were dedicated through sacrifice and prayer (with Moses, Solomon, the priests, and the people not able to enter, nor stand for that matter): so does Christ enter our hearts through sacrifice and prayer. His sacrifice, and our prayer to receive Him! We are now the Ark of God, the carriers of His presence!

We have become the Holy place for God Himself.

Now, in the Father's heart and mind, I could imagine:

"Now, this… this is what I have been waiting for. This was my plan all along. This is where I will call my rest; this is my Zion, my dwelling place, my sanctuary. These are my people, my church, my bride. This is My rest, forever."

> *"And Jesus saith unto him, The foxes have holes, and the birds of the air have nests; but the Son of man hath not where to lay his head." (Matthew 8:20)*

> *"LORD, remember David, and all his afflictions: How he sware unto the Lord, and vowed unto the mighty God of Jacob; Surely I will not come into the tabernacle of my house, nor go up into my bed; I will not give sleep to mine eyes, or slumber to mine eyelids, Until I find out a place for the Lord, a habitation for the mighty God of Jacob." (Psalm 132:1-5)*

That night, King David went to sleep. It is only the Lord Almighty who neither sleeps nor slumbers (Psalm 121:4). So, what was David saying here? Well, it wasn't David at all. Jesus was speaking *through* David, saying:

"I will not rest until I find my rest in you, my church."

> *"For the Lord hath chosen Zion; he hath desired it for his habitation. This is my rest for ever: here will I dwell; for I have desired it." (Psalm 132:13-14)*

No tent, temple, or Ark would suffice. His desired dwelling was not found on earth. Our hearts were always the homes He looked forward to.

Chapter Eight

Into Promise

"Go thy way, eat thy bread with joy, and drink thy wine with a merry heart; for God now accepteth thy works." (Ecclesiastes 9:7)

Behold, the promised land!

Each chapter thus far has been crucial in preparing us to reign in the land. Each step was vital in leading us to where we are now.

We wouldn't be here if not for the wilderness. Moreover, we couldn't have entered the wilderness if it hadn't been for our Exodus. Foremostly, we couldn't have exited Egypt without first having walked through the Door of the Lamb who was slain.

The promised land is where you have inherited your mountain as Caleb, and have submitted yourself to *Joshua*. You realized the giants were never your enemy, your unrenewed mind was. You've tasted and seen how the Lord was good, and in turn, you've anchored your soul and buffeted your body.

You have fixed your eyes on Jesus and have not gone back. Your heart was not a dwelling place for Egypt. It was a haven for God's will and ways. You may have been camping in the wilderness, but you were living in the promised land already.

You saw the giants as food, and yourself as the title-deed holder. The giants were trespassing on your mountain; the high place became the Lord's. You have patiently waited for Isaac; you are holding him in joy and laughter. You chose to trust God with all that you were and all that you would become. You decided that God had a better course for your life than you could've ever mapped out for yourself.

You are called by God and thoroughly equipped.

When it comes to preparation: You are as Paul and Barnabas separated unto the ministry. Trust: You are as Peter fast asleep on the night of his execution. Boldness: You are confident as Daniel praying out of his window, knowing the lions await. Assurance: You are steadfast as Stephen beholding the Son of man. Timing: You are as David in perceiving that God's given you the kingdom. Empowered: You are as Jesus walking on the water.

Through faith and patience, you have inherited Canaan, and through trust and rest, you have tasted of the milk and honey. You are eating of the first-ripe fruits of the land; you are partaking of the very promise.

You're running barefoot through the rich fertile soil! You're lifting your hands in joy! The oil and wine, your portion forever; the Bread of Life, your continual feast.

Jesus is your inheritance; Jesus is your finished work.

Takeover

"Nevertheless, David took the stronghold..." (2nd Samuel 5:7)

Who entered the promised land? Who led the charge? *Joshua.*

He has now taken us in. He was the pioneer that led the second generation into the land. Joshua's conquests were that of Jesus going through our soul and destroying each giant, stronghold, and enemy of our minds. As David, who restored Israel and tore down the high places in the land, so would the true mirror, Jesus, restore our land and tear down the high places of our souls.

The heart of man is the ground in which the promised land is settled. The soul is that of the surrounding mountains left to overtake. As previously mentioned, the possession of the promised land occurred before we ever entered in. The inheritance occurred the moment we asked Jesus to save our lives. Like the children of Israel came out of Egypt whole, we have *all* of Jesus. However, Jesus wants all of *us*.

As discussed throughout this book, a change in perspective was the goal in mind. It was not to provide another gospel or to show *another* way. It was only to show *His* way... the way He always intended. Unfortunately, in some cases, His way has turned into men's traditions, and in turn, has made God's word of none effect.

Through the intended context of each provided passage, this book has endeavored to reshape the way you see God. In order to accomplish this, a substantial amount of scripture was necessary. Since many have taken only one scripture to run with, it was essential to have provided enough for your reconsideration—all for the sake of the right perspective.

Arriving in this final chapter will be with the same approach and intent. A slight adjustment in perspective may be necessary.

This book's purpose was to prove how it has *always* been all about Jesus; what should change now? Could it be that the promised land is all about Him? And hopefully, I've convinced you that Jesus is all about you.

I would like for you to consider how the promised land may not be as distant as you may have thought. Take another look around, does it seem familiar? Perhaps you have already been here before... well, you have, because the promised land is *you*.

We are the land the Father promised to Jesus.

Let that sink in for a moment. It may be of some shock. You should reread it.

We are the land the Father promised to Jesus.

We are *His* promised land... We are the fruit of *His* labor. We are the whole field He purchased to redeem us as *His* treasure. We are the everlasting possession that Jesus wants to fully inhabit!

> *"And there remained among the children of Israel seven tribes, which had not yet received their inheritance. And Joshua said unto the children of Israel, How long are ye slack to go to possess the land, which the LORD God of your fathers hath given you?" (Joshua 18:2-3)*

The promised land is about Jesus inheriting all of us! It's about agreeing with *Joshua* and allowing His takeover. The fullness of our inheritance is more accurately viewed as His complete possession of us. Submission must be given; it cannot be taken. When we submit to Jesus, we're simply giving over the ground He rightfully purchased! The Father gave us the earnest of the Holy Ghost for the possession He purchased through Christ.

> *"In whom ye also trusted, after that ye heard the word of truth, the gospel of your salvation in whom also, after that ye believed, ye were sealed with that holy Spirit of promise, Which is the earnest of our inheritance until the redemption of the purchased possession, unto the praise of his glory." (Ephesians 1:13-14)*

Remember Abraham? Remember how the Lord promised him an everlasting inheritance? Could it be that the Father was speaking *through* him, rather than *to* him? Perhaps the Father was speaking to someone else? Let me provide some scriptures for a slightly adjusted perspective, one that takes your eyes off man and unto Jesus.

Through Abraham's belief, he ushered in the Seed of promise to eventually inherit all of us. Like Mary agreed with the Father's plan on earth, having a hand in delivering Jesus, Abraham was the mediator on earth that paralleled the Mediator to come. I believe God made a covenant with Christ on the day Abram fell asleep.

"And when the sun was going down, a deep sleep fell upon Abram; and, lo, an horror of great darkness fell upon him...And it came to pass, that, when the sun went down, and it was dark, behold a smoking furnace, and a burning lamp that passed between those pieces. In the same day the Lord made a covenant with Abram, saying, Unto thy seed have I given this land, from the river of Egypt unto the great river, the river Euphrates." (Genesis 15:12, 17-18)

Though Abraham was obviously involved, Jesus was the smoking furnace and burning lamp that passed between the pieces. God promised Jesus a multitude of nations for Him to inherit! When we say yes to Jesus' finished work, He then washes our field with blood, and sits as Governor of the land promised to Himself!

"Wherefore when he cometh into the world, he saith, Sacrifice and offering thou wouldest not, but a body hast thou prepared me: In burnt offerings and sacrifices for sin thou hast had no pleasure." (Hebrews 10:5-6)

Jesus' flesh was the body prepared by the Father, but we are the body prepared for Jesus. The Holy Ghost possessing us is His finished work!

To us, Jesus is our promise; but to Jesus, we are the promise of the Father.

"And, being assembled together with them, commanded them that they should not depart from Jerusalem, but wait for the promise of the Father, which, saith he, ye have heard of me." (Acts 1:4)

Now, it would be appropriate to say that the relationship is mutually beneficial. It's not so much a discussion of semantics, but perspective. The perspective I have of the promised land is that of a marriage. As a husband and wife become one, so is the promise of Christ and His church. And we are all the bride of Christ!

"This is a great mystery: but I speak concerning Christ and the church."
(Ephesians 5:32)

We must submit to Jesus, even as Sarah did unto Abraham calling him lord. We are all the bride of Christ. We are the womb in which He places His Seed. As a wife is the garden and land of her husband, so are we in relation to our Husband, Christ.

"For the eyes of the Lord run to and fro throughout the whole earth, to shew himself strong in the behalf of them whose heart is perfect toward him..." (2nd Chronicles 16:9)

The Lord is searching for a heart to overtake. Thank God we said yes! Jesus is who we've been searching for all along, and we are who He has been relentlessly seeking. He's been searching for our hearts! That's all He ever wanted. Now, for Him to have all of our heart, we must submit all of our soul.

The next string of scriptures will further prove the reality of Jesus possessing *His* land. He does it through our soul's portal. He does it through our soul's amen.

We often pray: *"Lord, I want more of You."*

I believe God's response is: "I want more of *you*."

We are co-laborers with Christ!

"For we are labourers together with God: ye are God's husbandry, ye are God's building." (1st Corinthians 3:9)

We must work together. The Lord is not going to overtake that which we do not agree with.

"Can two walk together, except they be agreed?" (Amos 3:3)

Jesus is standing at the door of our soul, knocking and asking to be let in:

"Lift up your heads, O ye gates; even lift them up, ye everlasting doors; and the King of glory shall come in." (Psalm 24:9)

I believe this Psalm is referring to Jesus being let into our soul. Our heart's door needs to open in order to let his glory overtake our whole being. He is asking:

"Will you let Me overtake this thought process? Are you willing to allow the light of My word transform you?"

Not as rules and regulations written upon stone, but as a loving Father walking Hand in hand with His children. He shines the light of His word upon the failing components of our souls.

Our spirits have been perfected, but our souls need to catch up! This only occurs by letting Jesus in!

"The spirit of man is the candle of the LORD, searching all the inward parts of the belly." (Proverbs 20:27)

"Nevertheless, David took the strong hold of Zion: the same is the city of David. And David said on that day, Whosoever getteth up to the gutter, and smiteth the Jebusites, and the lame and the blind, that are hated of David's soul, he shall be chief and captain. Wherefore they said, The blind and the lame shall not come into the house." (2nd Samuel 5:7-8)

We are Zion, and the stronghold the Lord has overtaken. There are aspects of our minds that are saying to the Lord: *"You can't enter!"*

Nevertheless, *David* (Jesus) took the stronghold.

There are lame and blind components in our souls that are not found in the soul of Christ. Jesus wants to mirror our soul with His.

This is the essence of the promised land in full: He desires to inherit all of us, not some of us. To the degree we allow His word to transform us, is to the degree we can rest in His finished work.

Jesus' reign in you can only be done from a position of rest. Each paragraph from this point forward will focus on the true rest of God.

Solomon had rest from war because of his father David's conquests. Solomon was a man of peace because David was a man of war. Solomon inherited a throne of peace because he was David's son! Likewise, we are partakers of the peace that was made through Jesus' bloody cross. We are as Solomon, *His church*, resting from the war that was won. Peace is our inheritance because of Jesus' labor.

The Rest, And The Journey

> *"At the commandment of the LORD they rested in the tents, and at the commandment of the LORD they journeyed: they kept the charge of the LORD, at the commandment of the LORD by the hand of Moses."* *(Numbers 9:23)*

I would like to provide some insight into how we allow Jesus' full habitation. The word of God produces rest. Our rest permits His conquering. Our rest enables His work.

The pillar of fire at night, and the cloud by day, was a monumental revelation shown to me by the Holy Spirit. In the ninth chapter of the book of Numbers, we can see how being led by the Spirit goes hand in hand with being at rest. They are one in the same.

When we become still and fix our eyes on Him, we negate all doubt and fear. If we are anxious, troubled, in distress, or in compulsion, we'll miss the still and peaceful voice of God. We must never move out of compulsion, or fear, but only from a peaceful draw of God's Holy Spirit.

> *"And let the peace of God rule in your hearts, to the which also ye are called into one body; and be ye thankful."* *(Colossians 3:15)*

If peace is to rule in our hearts, there can't be any *other* ruler. Choosing to have a heart full of peace is of the utmost importance when it comes to hearing God. According to the book of Hebrews, true rest will only come from knowing His word:

> *"Let us labour therefore to enter into that **rest**, lest any man fall after the same example of unbelief. For the **Word of God** is quick, and powerful, and sharper than any twoedged sword, piercing even to the dividing asunder of soul and spirit, and of the joints and marrow, and **is** a discerner of the thoughts and intents of the heart."* *(Hebrews 4:11-12) (emphasis mine)*

This is the reason the children of Israel were commanded to rest in their tents when the cloud tarried long. If we are not experiencing a peaceful desire orchestrated by the Holy Spirit to move, we need to be at rest where the Lord has pitched our tent.

"Or whether it were two days, or a month, or a year, that the cloud tarried upon the tabernacle, remaining thereon, the children of Israel abode in their tents, and journeyed not: but when it was taken up, they journeyed." (Numbers 9:22)

Knowing when to journey is tied to being at rest.
Numbers 9:15 and 16 says:

"And on the day that the tabernacle was reared up the cloud covered the tabernacle, namely, the tent of the testimony: and at even there was upon the tabernacle as it were the appearance of fire, until the morning. So it was alway: The cloud covered it by day, and the appearance of fire by night."

So it was always…
This is profound. For the forty years the Israelites encamped around the Ark of the Covenant, the cloud by day, and the pillar of fire by night, was always there. How remarkable! The cloud, and pillar of fire, is a typology of the Holy Spirit, and the Ark is a portrait of Christ. The *Ark* and the *Cloud* were in perfect agreement. Jesus and the Holy Spirit are in perfect unity!

"Then was Jesus led up of the Spirit into the wilderness to be tempted of the devil." (Matthew 4:1)

The Spirit led the word! Jesus didn't go where He wanted, He went where the Spirit led Him. When Jesus heard the news that Lazarus was sick, He remained in the town He was in two days longer. This event correlates well with the passage mentioned previously:

"Or whether it were two days, or a month…" (Numbers 9:22)

*"When he had heard therefore that he was sick, he abode **two days** still in the same place where he was." (John 11:6) (emphasis mine)*

We might have stayed still in fear, or may have run to Lazarus out of compulsion, but Jesus travelled from a place of rest.
He was at rest in His tent until the cloud moved Him.
On a side note, Jesus came upon Lazarus being dead for four days. Which proves, if He journeyed upon initially finding out Lazarus was sick, He would still have arrived two days after he died.

"Then said Martha unto Jesus, Lord, if thou hadst been here, my brother had not died." (John 11:21)

This wasn't true. Had Jesus left upon hearing the news, Lazarus would still have died. Jesus *knew* that he was going to die:

"These things said he: and after that he saith unto them, Our friend Lazarus sleepeth; but I go, that I may awake him out of sleep...Then said Jesus unto them plainly, Lazarus is dead." (John 11:11,14)

Some may say:
"You know, if you would have been there, everything would have been different!"
We may even say this over again in our minds... but we can't afford to think this way. We need to be led by the Spirit, not bound by regret.

To be clear, this is not to say that we should wait to heal the sick! Or that we need a word from God to preach the Gospel. He already said *go!* This is only to say that we are to be led from compassion and peace. Whether we are laying hands on the sick, or journeying from place to place, it must be from a position of rest.

Let's consider a few passages that align with the leading of the Holy Spirit:

"Howbeit when he, The Spirit of truth, is come, he will guide you into all truth: for he shall not speak of himself; but whatsoever he shall hear, that shall he speak: and he will shew you things to come." (John 16:13)

Jesus was the Son of God, and in the book of Romans, we are told who the sons of God are:

"For as many as are led by the Spirit of God, they are the sons of God." (Romans 8:14)

Jesus, hearing the leading of the Spirit:

"And the same day, when the even was come, he saith unto them, Let us pass over unto the other side." (Mark 4:35)

We, hearing the Spirit's leading:

"And thine ears shall hear a word behind thee, saying, This is the way, walk ye in it, when ye turn to the right hand, and when ye turn to the left." (Isaiah 30:21)

"If we live in the Spirit, let us also walk in the Spirit." (Galatians 5:25)

As Jesus was submitted to the Father, and the leading of the Holy Spirit on earth, so must we submit to Jesus and be led by the Holy Spirit as well. Those who are led by the Spirit are the sons of God.

The Tabernacle Of Christ

Moses built the Tabernacle according to the pattern shown to him in the mount: Jesus was the mobile Tabernacle of God according to the pattern and plan of the Father.

Jesus was the full picture.

The significant design of the Tabernacle and the manner the Israelites would journey was the perfect foreshadow of Christ. It was only by the leading of the pillar of fire by night, or the cloud by the day that the congregation would move. Where the cloud or pillar would rest is where the tent of the Testimony was pitched. Afterward, the congregation would encamp around the Tabernacle.

What an awesome depiction of Jesus!

Wherever the Spirit of the Lord would lead Him is where He pitched His tent! Where He rested is where all the multitudes encamped! The multitudes followed Jesus, just as the children of Israel followed the Ark.

Jesus is the sum of the Old Testament church in the wilderness.

As mentioned in the previous chapter, the Ark represents Jesus. So, the children of Israel were essentially commanded to camp around Him!

When reading of Jesus' earthly ministry, His company was clearly sought after. Everyone wanted to sit at His feet! We're to follow this example in seeking Jesus by camping around the word of God.

Consider Numbers 9:17:

"And when the cloud was taken up from the tabernacle, then after that the children of Israel journeyed: and in the place where the cloud abode, there the children of Israel pitched their tents."

See, it wasn't the Ark that was taken up with the cloud following. It was the other way around. This is important to understand. We don't just "journey" on our own and see if the Spirit will follow our decision. We're to reflect the plans already made for us in heaven.

Chapter Nine

What gives a child of God more pleasure than knowing His will? In my opinion, nothing at all. Knowing God and His will has been my life's pursuit!

How many conversations have you had with fellow believers, and either they, or you have asked:

"I just want to know God's will for my life! If only it were clearer. I just want to hear His voice! It would be so much easier if He would simply tell me."

However, God *has* made His will clear.

Concerning the root of Numbers, chapter nine, there are a few branches to discuss which are pertinent to our walk with God. Each one to speak of is similar yet distinct. Each will shine more light on the will of God for your life.

One branch off this tree is knowing God's will while resting in our tents. What do we do when we don't know the next step? I've heard it said:

"Until God opens the next door, praise Him in the hallway."

Praise is something God is worthy of all the time. Praise is a weapon:

"...And Jesus saith unto them, Yea; have ye never read, Out of the mouth of babes and sucklings thou hast perfected praise?" (Matthew 21:16)

"Out of the mouth of babes and sucklings hast thou ordained strength because of thine enemies, that thou mightest still the enemy and the avenger." (Psalm 8:2)

Praise also takes your eyes off the problem and sets them on the solution. It's easy to praise God when the door is open, but He is the door *and* the hallway!

"I will bless the Lord at all times: his praise shall continually be in my mouth." (Psalm 34:1)

"Rejoice in the Lord alway: and again I say, Rejoice." (Philippians 4:4)

Thankfulness and praise are God's will for us now and always. In the waiting, in the uncertainty, in the hallway, in the promise: God is worthy to be praised.

"In every thing give thanks: for this is the will of God in Christ Jesus concerning you." (1st Thessalonians 5:18)

What is God's will for your life? To be thankful. Thankfulness causes contentment in the waiting, and praising God will cause you to focus on what you're thankful for! A healthy cycle of gratitude and praise.

> *"**And when the cloud tarried long** upon the tabernacle many days, then the children of Israel kept the charge of the Lord, and journeyed not."* *(Numbers 9:19) (emphasis mine)*

What happens when the cloud tarries long? What do we do when winter seems to last forever? We thank God for snow.

I would like to segue into a brief testimony concerning satisfaction.

One day while working outside, it came near to lunchtime. For some reason, I said out loud:

"Lord, I thank you for my appetite, because you're going to fill it."

This stopped me in my tracks. I realized how food was enjoyable because we have a desire for it. Without an appetite, what good is lunch? The Lord began to show me how He places the appetite in our hearts to bring satisfaction.

How do we know what God spoke to us will come to pass? We know this because God placed the desire in our hearts!

> *"Delight thyself also in the Lord, and he shall give thee the desires of thine heart. Commit thy way unto the Lord; trust also in him; and he shall bring it to pass. (Psalm 37:4-5)*

As you delight yourself in the Lord, He begins to *give* you those desires. So, you can trust your desires because they are from God! Waiting a long winter season will not determine if what God spoke will happen or not, having the desire for it in the first place will. Don't ever doubt the desire the Lord placed in your heart; He is looking forward to bringing the satisfaction.

Why do mountain climbers enjoy what they do? Because there is a summit. Why do marathon runners train for months to run 26 grueling miles? Because there is a finish line. The Lord doesn't want us to climb mountains without a peak, or run a marathon in vain.

Granted... mountain climbers and long-distance runners do enjoy the journey. Nevertheless, they run or climb to finish.

> *"For he satisfieth the longing soul, and filleth the hungry soul with goodness." (Psalm 107:9)*

Satisfaction is from the Lord! Who would climb a mountain without a peak? Who would run without an end? Our Father is good, and He desires to satisfy us.

"...for he that cometh to God must believe that he is, and that he is a rewarder of them that diligently seek him." (Hebrews 11:6)

The winter season brings more of an appreciation for spring. We need to learn to enjoy and trust God in the winter because spring is coming! Whether we're in a long season, or short: our day to day life is that of being thankful, and resting in His word.

Anxious For Nothing

Another branch off the trunk is the compulsion to move while waiting. The Lord wants us to be at rest, *especially* when we feel obliged to move. This is the Lord working patience in our lives.

"Are we there yet? Are we there yet?"

As adults we may not say this like our children do, but we consider this in our minds quite often.

"Do not be anxious or worried about anything, but in everything [every circumstance and situation] by prayer and petition with thanksgiving, continue to make your [specific] requests known to God." (Philippians 4:6 AMP)

It's in the moment we feel like moving forward the most, that we need to take the biggest step back. Anxiety will say *now*, but peace will say *wait*. Compulsion will say:

"Kill Saul now!"

Peace will say:

"...As the Lord liveth, the Lord shall smite him [Saul]; or his day shall come to die; or he shall descend into battle, and perish." (1st Samuel 26:10 (Brackets mine))

God will place the kingdom in your hands by His, not yours. Compulsion will have you trading your birthright for stew. Impatience will have you birth Ishmael; peace will bring forth Isaac in the time appointed. Hearing God in the still and the small is the key to journeying; not in the whirlwind, the thunder, or fire.

If you know Christmas is coming, you can rest. If it's June 18th, and you're certain December 25th is going to come, you can be content in knowing it will shortly arrive. However, if you're not even sure Christmas is coming, you'll be anxious every day leading up to it. That's why the psalmist wrote:

"...trust also in him, and he shall bring it to pass." (Psalm 37:5)

You cannot rest if you don't trust God! If you trusted God for Christmas to come, you wouldn't worry about missing it. Trust is the key to rest. Worry will rob you of the present *and* the future:

"But godliness with contentment is great gain." (1st Timothy 6:6)

Branch Of Harvest

Lastly, the branch of knowing when to move is most important of all. If you are premature in your journey, you'll miss it, and if you're late, you'll miss it as well. Knowing the timing of God is essential to reaping a harvest.

To hear God's still voice, we must be still ourselves. Camping around the Ark, and getting to know Jesus is the will of God. Following Jesus, when He moves, is the fruit of knowing Him. Care and concern will try to rob us of our relationship with Christ and close our ears to the Truth.

In the gospel of Mark, it speaks about the word being choked:

"And the cares of this world, and the deceitfulness of riches, and the lusts of other things entering in, choke the word, and it becometh unfruitful." (Mark 4:19)

What happens when someone is choking? They can't speak. If the word is not being spoken, it's not being heard. Therefore, care is the enemy of us hearing and following Jesus. We must remain at rest in order to go where Jesus is going. Otherwise, we won't hear His directions. Being content in our tents while waiting, and praising God when our soul doesn't feel like it, is what we're called to do.

"Why art thou cast down, O my soul? Why art thou disquieted within me? hope in God: for I shall yet praise him, who is the health of my countenance, and my God." (Psalm 43:5)

Grounded

Wandering the wilderness is quite different than resting in our tents. We're not wandering while waiting. We're resting assured. Otherwise, when it's time to move, we'll have choked out the voice of the word in the first place. There is a saying I speak often, and it is:

"I would rather err on the side of the word than trying to follow the Spirit."

At first, that might sound strange, but allow me to explain. I know that if I'm beholding Jesus in His word, I'll know when to move. I'm more "spiritual" when the word is my focus.

If I'm camping around the Ark in rest, I won't miss the wind of the Holy Ghost. On the contrary, if I'm seeking the Spirit without being grounded in the word, I may go astray.

There are friends I've known that have gone into heretical doctrines because the "spirit" spoke to them. Had they been grounded in the word of God, they would have known that wasn't the *Holy* Spirit.

"Beloved, believe not every spirit, but try the spirits whether they are of God: because many false prophets are gone out into the world." (1st John 4:1)

The Holy Ghost will only agree with Jesus, and bring to remembrance the words that He spoke.

"But the Comforter, which is the Holy Ghost, whom the Father will send in my name, he shall teach you all things, and bring all things to your remembrance, whatsoever I have said unto you...Howbeit when he, the Spirit of truth, is come, he will guide you into all truth: for he shall not speak of himself; but whatsoever he shall hear, that shall he speak: and he will shew you things to come." (John 14:26, 16:13)

One of the purposes of the five-fold ministry is to expound upon Jesus.

"Till we all come in the unity of the faith, and the knowledge of the Son of God, unto a perfect man, unto the measure of the stature of the fulness of Christ: That we henceforth are no more children, tossed to and fro, and carried about with every wind of doctrine, by the sleight of men, and cunning craftiness, whereby they lie in wait to deceive." (Ephesians 4:13-14)

Knowledge of the Son of God will keep us from going spiritually astray. Knowing the Prince of Peace will cause us to be led by the peace of the Holy Ghost. Be confident in the word and confident in the Spirit. Both are in perfect agreement.

The First Journey

"And it came to pass on the twentieth day of the second month, in the second year, that the cloud was taken up from off the tabernacle of the testimony...And they first took their journey according to the commandment of the Lord by the hand of Moses. In the first place went the standard of the camp of the children of Judah according to their armies..." (Numbers 10:11, 13-14)

Judah led Israel's army after the cloud was taken up for the first time, and every journey following. Jesus is the leader of the tribe of Judah!

*"Thus were the journeyings of the children of Israel according to their armies, when they set forward...And they departed from the mount of the Lord **three days'** journey: and the ark of the covenant of the Lord went before them in the three days' journey, to search out a resting place for them." (Numbers 10: 28, 33) (emphasis mine)*

In chapter four, *Bitter Waters*, we pointed out the three-day journey to Marah. In numbers 10, the Lord also mentions a three-day journey to find a resting place. Judah led the charge in seeking out a resting place for the Ark, and it took three days! Jesus continuously speaks of the lengths He would travel to find His rest within us.

One thing to remember as well: Jesus is always leading the charge. He's going before you and paving the way. Every time the children of Israel would move, *Judah* was in the front.

Rest assured that God is for us. Therefore, *nothing* can be against us.

Speak Lord

"We have also a more sure word of prophecy..." (2nd Peter 1:19)

I have come to trust the leading of the Holy Ghost through the word of God. I'd like to write about one occasion in particular: He led me home by the pillar of fire.

I was sitting on my porch one day seeking the Lord for the summer season in Colorado. I was out there to specifically ask God if I were to move home or not. For clarification, I wasn't asking *to* leave. I was praying *if* I should. When I asked if I should stay or go, I experienced tremendous peace in moving back to Long Island. I communed in my heart with the Lord:

"Father, do you want me to go home now? Is it a few weeks from now? Is it at the end of the summer?"

As I prayed, a family reunion came to mind. I sensed to bring it up.

I asked:

"Lord, do You want me to drive home for the reunion and stay there?"

Upon this request, God overwhelmed me with His peace. I knew I was to go home at the end of the summer. Though I was convinced, I prayed once more:

"Father, I would like You to confirm this in Your word to me."

When I opened my Bible, *He* opened it to the book of Revelation. The first verse I read was this,

"...Grace be unto you, and peace, from him which is, and which was, and which is to come; and from the seven Spirits which are before his throne." (Revelation 1:4)

The only phrase I noticed from this scripture was, "Grace be unto you and peace."

Right away, He said to me:

"I've given you the peace to go home. I've placed that desire in your heart. Now, I am also giving you the grace to accomplish it. I am with you."

He gave me the peace *and* the grace; He spoke to me from the Cloud, and through the Ark. It was a unity that could not be broken. I shared this experience because I believe this is the way God leads us. We are to be anxious for nothing; we're to rest in our tents and camp around the word of God, and we're to be led by the Holy Spirit. If we follow this Biblical pattern, we'll then be following Jesus.

In conclusion, being thankful and grateful always, focusing on the word of God amid temptation, and camping around the word will cancel out all the noise. If these principles are followed, the result will be hearing the Lord clearly and moving forward in His perfect timing. How we spend our time in the waiting will determine if we can follow His lead.

Peace Be Still

Now that we discussed *how* to be led by the Lord let's discuss *what* God's peace is all about. There is a significant difference between natural peace and the peace Jesus speaks about. Jesus' peace is our reality. The peace of God is not circumstantial, it is *internal*. True peace will always come from a place within.

I'm not saying that when you're sitting by the lake on a perfect summer's day while sipping on a sweet iced tea, that you're not going to experience some form of peace. You'd be enjoying the beautiful day the Lord had made! However, this is not the kind of peace Jesus said He'd leave us with. This type of peace that's experienced from a favorable circumstance is external.

Yes, it's true how in life we'll experience "beautiful" days... but what good would all those days be if our soul within is troubled? We can be having a perfect day on the outside, but feel as if our whole world is ready to collapse within. These things should never be.

The Lord certainly placed a great emphasis on the prosperity of our soul when having Isaiah prophesy:

"Thou wilt keep him in perfect peace, whose mind is stayed on thee: because he trusteth in thee." (Isaiah 26:3)

All the best days on earth can never compare to having true peace within. One day with the Prince of Peace is better than a thousand days anywhere else.

The type of peace Jesus wants to be Captain of is when you're on what seems to be a sinking ship, yet fast asleep. Jesus spoke peace to the storm from a place of peace within. He was able to calm the raging sea because the waters were first still within Him. We must follow His example.

The problem that the disciples faced, (as accounted in the gospel of Matthew, Mark, and Luke), was how they considered their circumstance while in the ship, and not Jesus. The waves were on the outside, but Jesus was on the inside. The waters started to overtake the ship, but Jesus didn't do anything about it until they asked for His help.

Think about this: Jesus wasn't affected by the water while He was asleep, or when He awoke. Only His followers were.

For illustrative purposes: our body is the ship, inside the ship is our soul, and Jesus is at rest in our spirit. Jesus wants to overtake all three until He is Captain of the whole thing.

If they had recognized Who was at rest in their boat, they wouldn't have been troubled at all. I believe this account was written for our admonition. Jesus is within our ship! As He is resting within, so should we be. Look at what Jesus says about His peace:

> *"Peace I leave with you, my peace I give unto you: not as the world giveth, give I unto you. Let not your heart be troubled, neither let it be afraid." (John 14:27)*

The Comforter is given to us as a gift! Praise God! Only the true peace that's birthed forth by the Holy Ghost can put our soul to rest in Jesus. This is so important!

All this to say, we can experience tremendous difficulties while being untouched within. Only Jesus can provide us with this heavenly reality.

When it comes to God's kind of peace: It is not manufactured. It is not self-willed. It is not false, nor do you have to put on a show… it's the real deal. It is the very reason why Jesus said it was better for His disciples if He left so that He could make His residence within them. The Prince of Peace has called our home His own.

Rest For The Weary

Jesus was the water source of Jacob's well:

> *"Now Jacob's well was there. Jesus therefore, being wearied with his journey, sat thus on the well: and it was about the sixth hour." (John 4:6)*

Notice how Jesus was wearied from His journey and chose to sit atop Jacob's well. He was showing us that when we become weary in our journey, we need to rest in the water of God's source: Jesus. This way, we will "never thirst again."

> *"But whosoever drinketh of the water that I shall give him shall never thirst, but the water that I shall give him shall be in him a well of water springing up into everlasting life." (John 4:14)*

If we are trying to satisfy our weariness with anything other than the pure water of Christ, we will faint along the way. To sit atop Jacob's well is to yoke ourselves to Jesus.

"Come unto me, all ye that labour and are heavy laden, and I will give you rest. Take my yoke upon you, and learn of me; for I am meek and lowly in heart: and ye shall find rest unto your souls. For my yoke is easy, and my burden is light." (Matthew 11:28-30)

When we are yoked to the things of this world and are pulled left and right, we'll find ourselves in distress. This is because we are yoking our mind, will, and emotions to carnal things, and not to Christ. We'll then find ourselves overwhelmed, burdened, and full of care. Why? Because we're not *learning* of Jesus.

What we are called to do is learn of Him! This is our burden! Learning of Jesus will *always* produce life and peace. That's how we can tell if we are attaching ourselves to the right source. According to this scripture, the burden that Jesus offers produces rest. Only in the kingdom of God can a burden bring alleviation.

I have found that taking a seemingly small burden unto myself, can become nearly impossible. I wonder why this task cannot be completed, and I wind up either barely making it through, or giving up altogether.

"Because strait is the gate, and narrow is the way, which leadeth unto life, and few there be that find it." (Matthew 7:14)

The Lord has called us to a straight path with a light load. We are to be hedged in peace.

I have also learned that when yoked to a burden the Lord called me to, whether small or great, it emerged as life-giving! How could this be? This was only possible because the source of strength I tapped into was God's and not my own.

The key is laboring out of a place of rest within our soul so that we can remain at rest within our bodies.

We don't walk around life with physical burdens on our shoulders, or yoked to carts dragging in a field; we carry them in our minds. That's why Jesus said that in coming to Him, we'd find rest for our *souls*, not our *bodies*. The type of rest Jesus has to offer is internal. We cannot afford to be yoked to the things of this world. We must cast our cares upon Him because He cares for us.

The light burden of Christ will always produce rest for our souls, resulting in our physical bodies lining up with this reality within.

*"Beloved, I wish above all things that thou mayest prosper **and be in health**, even as thy soul prospereth." (3rd John 1:2) (emphasis mine)*

Health and physical prosperity come from a prosperous soul.

How do we enter God's true rest? We are king David's mighty men. We are the church of Jesus! How do we see victory? When becoming weary, we don't drop our swords. Rather, we have them cleave to our hands. Second Samuel 23:10 says: *"He arose, and smote the Philistines until his hand was weary, and his hand clave unto the sword: and the Lord wrought a great victory that day..."*

The Lord will bring a great victory only if the sword of the Spirit *remains* in your hands when weary!

The temptation to surrender or succumb to pressure may be overwhelming at times, but the victory is only found in the word of God being held on to. Be encouraged and stand strong, especially when weary. Remember, we inherit the promises through faith and patience.

What has God spoken to you? Let it cleave to your hand. Let the word become flesh. Let your hand and the word become one. Let there be no separation. Then, you will become a living epistle read of all men.

"And let us not be weary in well doing: for in due season we shall reap, if we faint not." (Galatians 6:9)

Yes, And Amen!

"For all the promises of God in him are yea, and in him Amen, unto the glory of God by us." (2nd Corinthians 1:20)

The promise is not the problem. The Lord has *already* fulfilled His promises. They are not yet to be fulfilled, but rather already accomplished. Here is the key: the promise is the constant, and the amen is the variable. To the degree that we agree with the promise, is to the degree we will see the promises become effective in our life.

The word *amen* means *truth, so be it*. All the promises are working and in effect, but if we do not agree with what has been promised, we will not partake of it. But we will partake! We will receive! We will overcome our unbelief with the truth, and the truth shall make us free!

"Whereby are given unto us exceeding great and precious promises..." (2nd Peter 1:4)

Some of the promises: abundant life, true love, lasting joy, abiding peace, genuine prosperity, overall health, wholeness, fullness, and righteousness; a new heart, a sane and clear mind, true holiness, and all good things working together! Whatever is causing us to *disagree* with these things must be cast out!

Meditate, speak, and imagine. Do not let the sacred place of your mind conceive a contradictory thought against what God has said about you. In the marriage bed of your mind, only allow the word of God to conceive. You must *yada* what God says about you! Like conceiving a child, so is the word conceiving in your mind.

You must *amen* above how you feel. Faith is not contingent upon your feelings, but only what is written.

You are equipped and well able. Christ has counted you faithful for ministry. However, He first called the ministry of reconciliation to you. He wants you to be set free so that you may live this abundant life together with Him. So, from that place of wholeness, you may freely give to others.

It Is Finished

"Sin, when it was finished, brought forth death; Jesus, when He was finished, brought forth Life; and that Life more abundantly."

Jesus cried: "*It is finished.*"

What was finished? Every care and temptation we will ever face has been faced already in His mind: It is finished. Every sickness and disease placed on His body, rather than on ours: It is finished. Every need, every worry, every concern… Jesus cried: It is finished.

"For consider him that endured such contradiction of sinners against himself, lest ye be wearied and faint in your minds." (Hebrews 12:3)

We must only consider Him.

"How am I going to get…" Consider Him.
"Lord, I just can't take it any…" Consider Him.
"I can't see how…" Consider Him.
"I can't…" Consider Him.
"I…" Consider Him.

Consider Him
"Lord."

"Lord, here I am."

"Lord, here I am looking to you."

You're considering Him…

"Lord, I'm fixing my eyes on you… You've already seen this coming!"

You're considering Him!

"You've known and met my needs before they've ever arose! You know all my thoughts and all my words before I utter them! You will perfect all that concerns me! Lord, here I am! I trust in You! I rest in You! It is finished!"

David Ravella

For more information contact:

David Ravella
C/O Advantage Books
P.O. Box 160847
Altamonte Springs, FL 32716
info@advbooks.com

To purchase additional copies of these books, visit our bookstore at:
www.advbookstore.com

Longwood, Florida, USA
"we bring dreams to life"™
www.advbookstore.com